A DICTIONARY OF
FABULOUS BEASTS

A DICTIONARY OF
FABULOUS BEASTS

RICHARD BARBER

and

ANNE RICHES

With Illustrations by Rosalind Dease

THE BOYDELL PRESS

First published 1971
Reprinted 1996

First published in paperback 1996
The Boydell Press, Woodbridge

ISBN 0 85115 685 1

The Boydell Press is an imprint of Boydell & Brewer Ltd
PO Box 9, Woodbridge, Suffolk IP12 3DF, UK
and of Boydell & Brewer Inc.
PO Box 41026, Rochester, NY 14604–4126, USA

British Library Cataloguing in Publication Data
A catalogue record for this book is available
from the British Library

This publication is printed on acid-free paper

Printed in Great Britain by
St Edmundsbury Press Ltd, Bury St Edmunds, Suffolk

INTRODUCTION

Hunting fabulous beasts has been an entertaining and often surprising occupation; the quarry we have pursued through poetry and fiction to its lair in mythology or heraldry has often made us smile at its antics. But before we smile, too, at the simplicity of the inventors of such fanciful creatures, it will be as well to look at something of the pedigrees of the beasts, and to see how, behind their monstrous shapes, they have a more serious face than we might expect.

To classify any one beast accurately, and to ascribe it to a particular process of myth, is wellnigh impossible. A dragon, for instance, will lead us through mythology, iconography, heraldry, popular fancy and the supernatural beliefs of primitive tribes, and even then we shall not have finished dissecting his various forms and shapes. Nor do the ordinary divisions and descriptions of academic anthropology begin to provide adequate categories; some of our beasts have reached us, it is true, through anthropological material, but others belong strictly to the history of learning. So, despite Robert Graves's recent plea for a systematic guide to the zoology of fable, our beasts are ranked in alphabetical order, though parallels and similarities are pointed out wherever possible.

The most fruitful source of creatures that never walked this earth is the conscious or semi-conscious process of mythmaking, whether in the Sumerian account of the Creation, or in an American *jeu d'esprit* inventing myths for the Wild West such as lumberjacks might have dreamt up. Creation myths are a recurring source of gigantic beasts of the imagination, whether primeval versions of familiar species or compounds of known creatures. It is arguable, at least, that some of the animals which entered myth as part of the legends about the days before man existed could conceivably be dim inherited memories of the last giant mammals of the Pleistocene era. Other natural phenomena such as earthquakes, eclipses and thunder, which were, if not beyond primitive man's experience, outside his comprehension, were explained by gigantic beings: dragons and bulls who caused earthquakes, the thunderbirds, the dragons who swallowed the sun.

When early civilisations came to depict these creatures, they usually did so by compounding an image out of a mosaic of real beasts, as in Sumerian and Assyrian bas-reliefs. These attempts to describe a belief often produced another imaginary animal. It is very possible that Alexander's physician, Ctesias, was describing such a carving when he talked of the unicorn, and the griffins, sirrushes and yalis all have a similarly sculptural pedigree. Stripped of their original mythical function by the barrier of language, they took on a purely natural aspect, although their original attributes were occasionally attached to them again after a time; and beasts which were too impossible for even the early naturalists were regarded as mere ornamental fantasies. So attempted descriptions of mythical but functional creatures produced either apparently real animals or fabulous, purposeless images.

Travellers' tales were the main source of information about much of the world until the 'expansion of Europe' in the sixteenth and seventeenth centuries. And such hearsay as reached medieval Christendom was far from reliable, even if well intentioned. Indeed, the most famous of all English medieval travellers, 'Sir John Mandeville', was a fabulous being himself, the invention perhaps of a monk with a lively imagination and some knowledge of geography. From their stories, often seriously meant, another flock of creatures were invented, usually real enough at bottom, but described in a series of most unscientific similes, which made up in vividness what they lacked in accuracy. Camelopards and abaths were added to the fauna of Asia and Africa; and if they sound far more intriguing than giraffes and rhinoceroses to modern ears, it is only because scientific familiarity with the latter has bred a gentle contempt for mysteries.

But medieval travellers had little hope of accuracy when medieval science, or rather learning, was dedicated to showing that each part of creation contained a lesson from which sinful mankind could well profit. The bestiaries or books of beasts began as a late classical treatise on animals and birds, the Physiologus. Very early in the currency of the Physiologus, series of morals were tagged on, and from then on the cat was belled until the Renaissance. The book of beasts did not contribute much that was original; the great reverence for tradition and authority that helped medieval men to hold fast in an uncertain age meant that the contents stayed much the same, and Aristotle and Pliny would have learnt little from a fourteenth-century monk; indeed, they would have been able to remind him of much forgotten lore.

From the bestiaries, the idea of animals as symbols moved into the secular world of heraldry, where the need for new badges bred a whole host of fresh compound-creatures, from calygreyhounds to the wonderful pig of the ocean. We have come full circle: once again there is no pretence that the beast exists, but each creature has a definite function, to denote a quality or describe an attribute in pictorial terms.

All this was a sore trial to the savants of the Renaissance, trying to put back some classical order into the rich confusion of the world bequeathed to them by medieval piety. Slowly they discovered that a few doubts, such as Herodotus's misgivings about griffins, were in order, even if a real bishopfish or dragon were shown to them. Aldrovandus, in the early seventeenth century, realised how a convincing dragon could be fashioned from a skate; and many of the curiosities which furnished princely collectors' cabinets were scrutinised with a keener eye and found wanting. The dying embers of medieval enthusiasm for the unquestioned rarity still glow in such books as Lycosthenes's *Chronicle of prodigies and marvels* (1557), and as late as 1652 in Alexander Ross's *Arcana microcosmi*, a refutation of Sir Thomas Browne's *Vulgar Errors*. But it was Browne's sceptical turn of mind that was the spirit of the age. His third book 'Of divers popular and received tenets concerning animals, which examined, prove either false or dubious', is fearless of established authority; with his first salvo he demolishes the belief that the elephant has no joints and sleeps standing up, 'which conceit is not the daughter of later times, but an old and gray-headed error, even in the days of *Aristotle* . . . and stands successively related by several other authors: by *Diodorus Siculus, Strabo, Ambrose, Cassiodore, Solinus,* and many more. Now herein methinks men much forget themselves, not well considering the absurdity of such assertions.'

And so the picturesque zoo of medieval travellers and theologians was examined item by item and gently but firmly discarded. Only literary or accidental inventions swelled the ranks of the fauna of the imagination, and these were not always of the highest originality. The 'fearsome critters' of North America, although to some extent independently invented, have a curious habit of imitating earlier traditions: the hoop snake,

7

tail in mouth, is not unlike the Egyptian symbol of eternity, the hodag resembles both Pliny's achlis and the jointless elephant, and the goofang is an echo of the acipenser. They earn their place here as examples of folk humour; and the guyascutus has a genuine place in folklore.

Indeed, what to include and what to reject has been one of the chief problems in compiling this book. It is, in the end, a selection of fabulous birds, beasts and fishes, with a few fabulous beings thrown in. Anything entirely human has been excluded, though superhuman and subhuman beings appear. And every creature listed has some reasonably recognisable form: there are no entirely spiritual beings, though there are many spirits in corporeal guise. Finally, real animals only appear if the description of them is such as to mislead the casual observer into thinking them fabulous, for instance, the camelopard and the amphisbaena. One new beast was almost generated by the writing of the book, when, in the first draft, Aquarius the water-bearer appeared as Aquarius the water-beaver. And there is always the wayzgoose.

Abaia A great eel featuring in Melanesian mythology. His paternal care for the fish who shared his lake was so strong that whenever any fish were caught he caused a deluge.   (487)

Abath Found in the Malay peninsula according to a sixteenth-century traveller, the abath was a beast who had only one horn in its forehead. It was thought to be the female UNICORN, and was very highly esteemed by the Moors, who prized its horn as the ultimate remedy for all poisons. Trade in the horns was a royal monopoly. Its original in real life was the Asian rhinoceros, whose horn is still regarded by the Chinese as a powerful love-potion when ground and dissolved in wine.   (310)

Achelous A river-god figuring in Greek mythology, capable of assuming any form at any given moment, but commonly found in three guises, as a bull, a speckled serpent or a bullheaded man. In the latter form he was involved in a combat with Hercules and lost a horn. The drops of blood which fell from the horn became the SIRENS, but the horn itself was found by the naiads, who filled it with flowers; it was adopted as the symbol of plenty, hence cornucopia. When not disguised, Achelous could be recognised by streams of water flowing continually from his shaggy beard, and by his green weedlike clothing.

Achiyalabopa A bird-monster revered by the Pueblo Indians as a celestial god or a galaxy. It had feathers like knives.   (488)

Achlis A creature described by Pliny, it was not unlike an elk, but it lacked joints in its hind-legs; consequently it could never lie down, but reclined against a tree in order to sleep. The only way to capture it was by previously cutting into the tree, so that both it and the tree fell to the ground, as it was too swift to be taken by any other means. Another curious feature was its upper lip, which was so enormous that in order to graze it had to move backwards, because if it went forwards the lip would double up. See also HODAG. (118)

Acipenser The curious feature of this fishlike creature was that its scales were turned towards the head, with the result that it could never bear to swim against the stream. It is sometimes described as a sturgeon. Compare also GOOFANG. (459)

Aeternae Beasts found in India and so named because of their youthfulness. They had saw-edged bones like swords on their foreheads which they used in combats to pierce through shields. It was unwise to provoke one of the creatures to battle, as the soldiers of Alexander the Great were reputed to have done to their cost. (408)

Afanc A spirit representing the power of water, which appeared as a huge hairy man on a gigantic horse, cf. WATER-HORSE. It seems to have been a demon of the Celtic fringe, being found in Wales and Scotland. In *The Romance of Peredur* the Afanc lives in a cave at the door of which is a stone pillar. It can see everyone that comes without anyone seeing it; and from behind the pillar it uses a spear to kill any living creature that approaches, until it is ultimately slain by Peredur. It was, however, a more common belief that these spirits could not be slain with the sword, and the only way to render them harmless was to drag them from their watery habitat, or move them to new lands. Thus the Conway afanc was captured after being lured to the bank by the treachery of a girl it fell in love with. It was then dragged by oxen into one of the highest tarns on Snowdon, where it could no longer slay passers-by. (413, 496)

Ahuizotl A creature about the size of a dog with monkey's hands and feet and a hand on the end of a very long flexible tail, found in Mexico. It craved for human eyes, teeth and nails, which it acquired by seizing men with the hand on its tail. After vanishing for three days the corpses reappeared minus the relevant parts; they could only be touched by a priest because it was believed that the rain-gods had chosen those particular souls for paradise. Its other means of trapping humans was to sit on a river bank and cry like a child to attract attention; when humans approached it would strike them with its deadly tail. (470)

Aido Hevedo A rainbow serpent which helped to create the universe in Dahomey myth. It lived under the earth and was periodically cooled from the intense heat by the sea; it fed on a diet of iron bars, but when the supply ended it would devour its own tail and ultimately fall into the sea. Its movements (as with other world-supporting creatures) were the cause of earthquakes: cf VARAHA. (470)

Aigamuchas A creature which lived in the Kalahari desert with eyes on the top of its feet and thin pointed teeth as long as a man's finger. If these creatures wanted to know what was happening behind them they went on hands and knees with one foot lifted so that they could see backwards. They hunted men as if they were zebras and ate them. (484)

Aitvaras A Lithuanian flying dragon which was a good household spirit. It was hatched from the egg of a seven-year-old cock, in the same way as a BASILISK. When flying it appeared as a cock, except that it had a fiery tail. It carried wealth (usually stolen) to the household, and in return had to be fed on omelette. It could be slain, but only by mistake. (470)

Aja Ekapad A one-footed goat in Vedic myth, representing lightning. The goat was a symbol of swiftness, and hence of the lightning's flash, and its one foot of a single place of striking. (484)

Aker A double-headed earth-god of early Egyptian myth in the form of a lion with a man's head at each end. (490)

Al An impure spirit with fiery eyes, half-animal, half-beast, found in North Africa. These spirits held a pair of iron scissors in their hands, and wandered around or sat and contemplated in sandy places. They were disease-demons, who attacked women in childbirth. (483)

Al Borak or **Buraq** The milk-white steed of Mohammed which carried the prophet when he visited the seven heavens by night. It is described as a creature somewhere between a horse and an ass, often with wings. It traverses the earth with gigantic strides, each one of which is equal to the furthest range of human vision. Indian paintings of it show it with a man's face, ass's ears, a horse's body and peacock's plumage.

(410, 459)

Alan Philippine spirit, half-human, half-bird, who lived in forests in houses of gold, and hung batlike from the trees. These spirits were friendly but mischievous creatures. (470)

Alcyoneus A mighty ass which was probably the spirit of the sirocco wind. See TYPHON.

Alicha or **Arakho** (originally **Râhu** in India) A beast in Siberian mythology which lived in the heavens and swallowed the sun and the moon at intervals. It was cut in half by the gods, and the hind part fell to

the earth; the fore part remained in the sky and continued to swallow stars, but they quickly reappeared, as it could not keep them in its body. When Alicha was troubling the sun and moon (i.e. causing an eclipse) the Buriat people would throw stones and shoot at the sky to keep it away. See also DRAGON. (484)

Allerion An heraldic bird represented as an eaglet without beak or claws, occasionally found in a much smaller form, like a martlet. Perhaps derived from YLLERION. (515)

Allocamelus Heraldic creature with the body of a camel and the head of an ass. (515)

Aloadai In Greek myth, the Aloadai were Otos and Ephialtes, the sons of Poseidon and Iphimedia, who grew a cubit in breadth and a fathom in height every year. At the age of nine they determined to fight the gods and piled Pelion on Ossa to reach heaven. They were slain by Artemis, who became a deer and leapt between them; they took aim at her and fired, but killed each other instead. See also GIANTS. (103)

Alphyn An heraldic beast: although it looks like a tiger, the alphyn stems from the Arabic chess piece called *al-fil*, usually represented as an elephant, which is the equivalent of our knight. (474)

Altion see HALCYON.

Amarok A giant wolf believed in by the Eskimos. (488)

Ambize (Angulo or **Hog Fish)** A Congolese fish monster with the body of a fish, muzzle of an ox, two hands and a tail shaped like a target, which lived off a diet of grass; it grew to about five hundred pounds weight and tasted of pork. (321)

Ammut An ancient Egyptian monster of the underworld, partly hippopotamus, partly lion, with jaws like a crocodile. She was stationed by the scales of judgement in the hall of Osiris. She ate the hearts of all those who were burdened with sin. (470)

Amphiptere A winged serpent occasionally found in heraldry. (439)

Amphisbaena A two-headed creature, sometimes shown with feathers, but described as a snake by Pliny and by Lucan in his description of the terrors of the African desert in the *Pharsalia*. When one head was asleep, the other remained awake, particularly while hatching eggs; in this case the head on duty woke up the other one when it was time for it to take over. Curiously enough, it proves to be a real animal, a limbless lizard which can move both backwards and forwards, and which rears its tail if frightened, pretending that it is a second head. (228)

Analopos An animal found near the Euphrates which could only be captured by luring it into a thicket, where it entangled its horns. Similar to the APTALEON, both are probably antelopes. (228)

Anaskelades Supernatural donkeys found in Crete. According to modern folklore they appeared as a bobbin lying in the road; if anyone tried to pick it up, it would roll away and turn into a donkey. Should the inquisitive onlooker try to mount it, it would become as tall as a mountain and throw him down from a great height. A similar story is told about CALLICANTZARI. (468)

Anaye The Anaye or Alien Gods of Navaho Indian myth are giants and monsters born of women without intervention of men. They include Thelgeth, who was headless and hairy, Tsanahale, harpy-like with feathered back, the Binaye Ahani, twins without legs or arms who slew with their eyes, and a nameless monster whose hair grew into the rock so that it could not fall from the cliff where it lived, and which preyed on travellers. They were all slain by the son of the water and the son of the sun, except for Old Age, Cold, Poverty and Famine; these were allowed to live on, lest men should cease to honour the gods who protected them against these woes. (488)

Angels and **Archangels** Winged creatures with human forms; an angel was the name of an office, not of an order of being. They were messengers – ἄγγελος meant simply this in Greek – and Gabriel was thus the heavenly 'messenger' who appeared to Mary. They are depicted as

14

young to imply continued strength, winged to show tirelessness, without sandals to show that they do not belong to the earth, girded to show that they are ready to go out and execute God's work. Their white and gold clothing symbolises purity and sanctity. Archangels were frequently portrayed in armour. *Fallen Angels* take the form of satyrs with horns, hooves and tail. Their fall did not benefit them, for they became the devil's slaves, particularly in his form as the dragon of the apocalypse.   (515)

Angka   The Arabian name for the SIMURGH, though in some accounts it resembled a griffin. In this form it was thought to have been created by God to destroy wild beasts in Palestine, which it effectively did, leaving only the barren wastes of the wilderness.   (222)

Angulo, *see* AMBIZE

Anthias   According to Aelian these were sea fishes whose spirit of comradeship was so strong that if they became aware that one of their kind had been hooked they would swim up swiftly, and by setting their backs against it and pushing as hard as they could, they would try to stop it being hauled in.   (101)

Ant-Lion   The ant-lion had the countenance of a lion and the hind parts of an ant. His father was a carnivore, his mother a vegetarian. When they produced the ant-lion, he was born with both attributes, and consequently died because there was no food suitable for him. Other authorities say that he hid in the dust and killed ants which carried grain; he acquired his name because he was a lion among ants and an ant among lions. The creature arose out of a mistranslation of Job iv 11: 'The old lion perisheth for lack of prey', because the Septuagint uses a rare word for the Arabian lion, *myrmex*, whose meaning was later forgotten. Hence the original name *mirmecoleon*; also called *formicoleon*.   (204, 228)

Ants, Ethiopian   Solinus describes these as creatures particularly skilled in digging for gold. They were the size of dogs and very vicious, attacking anyone who dared encroach on their territory. If a man was foolish enough to attempt to steal any of their jealously guarded hoard, he was immediately devoured. The only creatures tolerated by these ants were mares that had just foaled. If these mares were driven across the river bordering the ant's country with panniers on their backs, the ants would hide gold in these containers, and the mares, when they had eaten their fill of lush grass, would return to their foals, bearing the treasure with them. (119)

Anubis Jackal-headed god of the ancient Egyptians, judge and lord of the dead: he weighed the hearts of the dead in the scales of the Last Judgement, and led the wicked to their place of punishment. (490)

Apis A black bull worshipped by the Egyptians at Memphis, with white marks resembling eagle's wings on his forehead and back. Under his tongue was a hump in the shape of a scarab. He was kept in a building facing east and fed on milk for four months before being taken with great ceremony down the Nile to Memphis, where he acquired a temple and sacrifices were made to him. The anniversary of his birth was celebrated as a festival each year. If he lived over twenty-five years he was drowned in the sacred cistern. When he died he was buried at Saqqarat and mourned for seventy days, at the end of which time a new calf was 'found'. (417)

Apop Serpent of the abyss, or ocean-serpent which lies in darkness, in Egyptian mythology, derived from Tiamat and Bel-Marduk in Babylonian myth. The enemy of the sun-god, whose solar disc he swallowed, he was killed by the cat-god in some versions of the myth; in an Osiris hymn, Horus binds him and Osiris hews him in pieces. (490)

Apotharni According to Conrad Wolfhart's *Chronicle of Prodigies and Apparitions* these were a tribe which were half-men, half-horses; cf. CENTAURS. The females were always bald, but grew beards. They dwelt in watery places. (315)

Apres A bull with a short tail like a bear found, though very occasionally, in heraldry. An apres is the sinister supporter of the arms of the Muscovy Company. (515)

Apsaras In Brahmin myth, water-nymphs with very beautiful faces and bodies who sometimes transformed themselves into water-fowl. They loved to sing and dance, with the result that they were skilled musicians. They were forced to associate with gandharvas, Hindu gods of the atmosphere, and extended their favours to warriors who had fallen in battle and had therefore entered the paradise of Indra. (484)

Apsu, *see* TIAMAT

Aptaleon A Babylonian beast with two serrated horns and a goat's body. He had a habit of cutting down great trees with his horns, which produced a great thirst. He quenched this from the waters of the Euphrates and went off to play in a bush called an erechire; this bush trapped him by the horns and held him fast. This creature was probably an antelope. See also ANALOPOS, CALOPUS. (225, 228)

Arakho, *see* ALICHA

Areop-Enap The Ancient Spider in the creation myth from Nauru in the South Pacific who made earth and sky by opening a giant mollusc with the aid of two snails and a worm. The two snails became the sun and the moon; the worm, Rigi, opened the mollusc's shell and his sweat became the salt sea as he pushed the two halves open. In other versions of the myth, Rigi was a butterfly who flew between earth and sea to separate them. Areop-Enap's son Areop-It-Eonin, Young Spider, created fire by bringing it from the house of thunder and lightning. (487)

Argopelter A hoary American beast which lived in the hollow trunks of trees; it passed its time by throwing splinters and lumps of wood at unsuspecting passers-by, who were sometimes quite seriously hurt. It never allowed itself to be seen. See FEARSOME CRITTERS. (412)

Argus A hundred-eyed monster of Greek mythology. His eyes slept two at a time until Mercury charmed him to sleep with his Pan pipes in order to slay him and free Io, Jupiter's mistress. Juno used his eyes to decorate the peacock's tail. (113)

Arimaspi A one-eyed tribe found in Scythia, who coveted the gold hoarded by griffins: Herodotus was prepared to accept the existence of the griffins, but was dubious about one-eyed men. (107)

Arion The winged horse of Adrastus in Greek legend. Cf. PEGASUS.

Arrak (early-wake) and **Alsvid** (all-strong) Horses of the sun's chariot in Scandinavian myth. See HORSES OF THE SUN. (480)

Asho-Zushta In the myths of the Zoroastrians of Persia, a bird which recited the Avesta, their sacred texts, which he had on his tongue, and put fiends to flight. When a Zoroastrian cut his nails he had to say, 'O Asho-zushta bird, these nails I present and consecrate to thee. May they be for thee so many spears and knives, so many bows and eagle winged arrows, so many sling stones against the Mazainyan demons.' If the spell was not said the fiends would use the nails against the bird and kill it. (484)

Ass, Three-Legged Creature from the Zoroastrian mythology of Persia. The *Bundahish*, a ninth-century text, describes how, when Tishtrya purified the earth of evil beings before the appearance of man; he did so by a shower of rain which became the sea, Vourukasha. In this he was aided by a three-legged ass. 'It stands amid the wide-formed ocean, and its feet are three, eyes six, mouths nine, ears two, and horn one, body white, food spiritual, and it is righteous. And two of its six eyes are in the position of eyes, two on the top of the head, and two in the position of the hump: with the sharpness of these six eyes it overcomes and destroys. Of the nine mouths, three are in the head, three in the hump, and three in the inner part of the flanks; and each mouth is about the size of a cottage, and it is itself as large as Mount Alvand. . . . When that ass shall hold its neck in the ocean its ears will terrify and all the water of the wide-formed ocean will shake with agitation. When it pisses in the ocean all the sea water will become purified' otherwise 'all the waters in the sea would have perished from the contamination which the poison of the evil spirit has brought into its water.' Possibly related to the one-legged Chinese K'NEI, it may have influenced descriptions of the Japanese KUDAN. (484)

Ass-Bittern A compound animal-bird very occasionally found in heraldry.

Atargatis or **Derceto** Semitic moon-goddess who, in a late Greek version of her myth, became the first MERMAID. Atagartis gave birth to Semiramis, but was so ashamed of her action that she in expiation killed her lover. She took a fish's form, while retaining certain human characteristics. For this reason, the Syrians would not eat fish. (517)

Attagen A singing bird referred to in Elizabethan literature which never sang again once it had been captured. (497)

Avanc, *see* AFANC

Bagwyn A heraldic beast first recorded in heralds' visitations *c.* 1540. It has the tail of a horse and the horns of a goat which are curved backwards. (474)

Baku A Japanese creature, not unlike a tapir in appearance, which feeds on the bad dreams of the human race; such dreams must be offered to it with the words 'Devour, o Baku!' (463)

Balios and **Xanthos** Immortal horses of Greek myth who drew the chariot given by Poseidon to Pelops.

Bandersnatch Described by Lewis Carroll as having savagely snapping 'frumious' jaws, with a recommendation that it should be avoided (frumious means 'furious-fuming'). The banker was attacked by one during the hunting of the SNARK.

Banshee A spirit of Irish and Scottish legend, sometimes known in Scotland as the Little Washer of Sorrow. She had only one nostril, a large projecting front tooth and long streaming hair. She also had webbed feet, presumably because she spent her life by the river where she could be heard constantly wailing, while washing the clothes of a man destined to die. This continual weeping had given her fiery red eyes. If she was captured by a mortal while washing in the river she had to divulge the name of the man doomed to die, and then grant three wishes. In Irish legend the banshee only wailed for members of the old-established families. In Scotland the banshee/banshi was a fairy woman who had a particular tendency to marry a mortal. (413)

Baobhan Sith An evil spirit particularly found in isolated parts of Scotland. There was a tribe of these spirits which sometimes appeared as hooded crows, but more commonly they were seen as beautiful girls with long trailing green dresses which hid their deer's hooves. They lured young men into their company and then sucked their blood. A particularly horrible instance of their evil ways is related in a Ross-shire tradition: four men out hunting were entertained by four baobhan siths; only one realised his peril in time and escaped to tell the tale. (413)

Baphomet A symbol attributed to the Templars, which was supposed to feature in mysterious rites practised by them. It was probably a rather unsubtle version of Mahomet dreamed up by their accusers in the trials of 1307–10, after which the order was suppressed. The baphomet is found in continental heraldic devices (but not in British) and is depicted as a female with two heads, one male, the other female. (515)

Bar Yachre A creature possibly related to the ROC. Found in very ancient Jewish legends and reported by Marco Polo in the accounts of his travels through the Middle East. See GRIFFIN. (222)

Bargvest Spirit of Celtic mythology usually appearing in the form of an animal, but occasionally in human form. It had eyes like burning coals, claws, horns and a tail, and was girdled with a clanking chain. This spirit appeared particularly in fishing villages; if it died and there was a bargvest funeral, this was seen by the fishing community as a portent of impending tragedy. In Yorkshire they were said to haunt the neighbourhood of churchyards. (413)

Barnacle Geese or **Ephemerus**   These sea birds, resembling common wild geese but smaller, found mainly off the north-western coasts of
the British Isles, were supposedly produced in a most extraordinary
manner. The barnacle goose was born from pine wood which had been
steeped in salt water. There were no eggs; the birds were never known
to pair or build nests. The first sign of these birds were gummy excrescences on the pine wood floating on the sea. These became enclosed
by shells and they appeared to develop beaks and hang from the timber

with them as if they were seaweed. As time passed they grew feathers,
and when fully developed the shells opened like wings and the birds fell
into the water or flew away. If they fell on to land they died. These birds
first appear in literature in the twelfth and thirteenth centuries, though
pictures dating from before 800 B.C. have been found on pottery at
Mycenae. Alexander Neckham and Gerald of Wales were the first to
catalogue them. Mandeville saw them on his travels; Aeneas Sylvius
Piccolomini, later Pope Pius II, while visiting James I of Scotland inquired

after the barnacle geese, and reputedly commented that 'miracles flee further and further'. Holinshed, also in the sixteenth century, reports the barnacle goose.

Because these birds were not born from eggs it became common practice to eat them in Lent. This led to a clerical scandal in the thirteenth century, culminating in a Papal bull forbidding the consumption of barnacle geese in Lent. The barnacle goose has sometimes been related to the symbolism of baptism, i.e. it was necessary to fall into the water to be born again. The barnacle goose tree has been likened to the tree of life, from which shining shells fall into the sea of tribulation, and subsequently by the grace of God are given wings and fly to heaven.

There are very many varieties of name for this bird: Brantas, Bernicles, Bernichlas, Bernekke, Barhatas, Bernestas, Barbatas, Clakis, Clacuse, Claiks, Clarkgeese are a few examples.

The appearance of the barnacle goose is probably an early explanation of migrating birds, which were never seen to mate, nest or hatch out eggs, as they only appeared in the north in the winter when they were in their adult or near-adult state. Both bird and barnacle are real enough; it is only the spurious connection between them in medieval nature-lore that produced a fabulous creature.   (212, 220, 452)

Barometz, *see* VEGETABLE LAMB OF TARTARY

Barrow-Wight or **Haug-Bui** Substantial ghosts associated in the Anglo-Saxon period with Bronze Age barrow graves, thought by some to be the inhabitants of the barrow who attacked anyone attempting to remove the treasure. St Guthlac, who lived in a barrow in Cambridgeshire, was continually having to defend himself from these creatures, who were described by his biographer as follows: 'They had great heads, long necks and lean faces; they had filthy squalid beards, rough ears, distorted countenances, fierce eyes and foul mouths; their teeth were like the teeth of horses, their throats were filled with flame and they had grating voices; they had crooked shanks, knee-joints bent backwards and toes to front; their voices were hoarse and they came with such an immoderate din and such immeasurable horror that it seemed to St Guthlac that all between heaven and earth resounded with their fearful noise.' Other sources aver that they could only be killed by cutting off their heads and then placing them at their knee. Anyone who saw a barrow-wight either went mad or was killed by them. (437)

Basadae A monstrous tribe of men found in India, they were very contorted with skins so thick that no arrow would ever penetrate them. Their various forms included men with dogs' heads, men with one leg and men with one eye. A peculiar attribute of this tribe was that by eating the heart and liver of a dragon they were able to understand the language of animals. They could also make themselves invisible. The tribe never lacked liquid refreshment, as they could produce water and wine themselves. (306)

Basilisk or **Cockatrice** This, the most deadly of all creatures, appears in the form of a small serpent, scarcely six inches long. According to Pliny, it has a whitish marking on the crown of its head strongly resembling a diadem, which singles it out as king of all serpents. When it moves, half its body slides along the ground in the normal reptile manner, but the front section is carried upright and erect. When it hisses all

creatures take flight, for if they remain within its range even a glance will mean certain death. Whatever comes in contact with its venomous breath perishes, whether it be man, beast, fowl or plant, and it dwells in the desert it has created. There were only three things which spelt doom for the basilisk: a weasel, a cock crowing and the sight of its own reflection in a mirror. In the last case, the basilisk was slain by its own glance, a borrowing from the legend of the GORGON Medusa. The mirror was still commonly believed to be the surest way to destroy the basilisk in the sixteenth century. The only creature which dared attack him was the weasel, and it was possible for a weasel to slaughter a basilisk although the weasel itself always died in the struggle. It was believed by medieval writers that the basilisk was hatched from an egg laid by a seven-year-old cock, when the dog star Sirius was in the ascendant. The egg was spherical and had to be hatched by a toad, a process which tradition held could take as long as nine years. Occasionally the basilisk and cockatrice are given separate identities, the basilisk remaining more completely a reptile, while the cockatrice retained its feathers and was sometimes said to have painted wings and a tail curving over its back. The basilisk is found in many parts of the western world: Pliny says it comes from the province of Cyrene, but it is found in numerous other places, Libya being one, where travellers always carry a cock for protection.

The basilisk appears frequently in literature; Chaucer and Spenser refer to him, and in *Richard III* Edward's widow Anne cries, as Richard woos her and praises the beauty of her eyes: 'Would they were basilisks to strike you dead!'

In a biblical context the basilisk is chiefly characterised by its venomous sting or bite, and in such guise is symbolic of the Devil. Jeremiah (viii 17) says, 'I shall send serpents, cockatrices among you which will not be chained, and they shall bite you, saith the Lord.' Innumerable strange tales surround the basilisk. It was commonly believed in the Middle Ages that if you struck one from horseback with a spear the poison would immediately rise through the spear and kill both man and horse. When a basilisk was killed, according to Greek legend, it lost all its deadly powers, and was hung in the temple of Apollo and in private houses, where it would merely frighten spiders away. The basilisk appears frequently in heraldic devices. See also CATOBLEPAS, GORGON, SKOFFIN.

(101, 118, 206)

Bayard An immortal horse belonging to the four sons of Aymon, which grew or shrank depending on the size of the rider. (459)

Behemoth Sometimes identified as a hippopotamus (and perhaps derived from the Egyptian hippopotamus goddess Taurt mentioned by Herodotus), it is described in the book of Enoch (lx, 7–9) in the Apocrypha as follows: 'And in that day will two monsters be separated, a female named Leviathan to dwell in the abyss over the fountains of waters. But the male is called Behemoth which occupies with his breasts an immeasurable desert named Dendain.' According to Moslem tradition, God created the earth, and it was not secure; so he placed below it first an angel, then a rock made of ruby, than a bull with four thousand eyes, ears, nostrils, mouths, tongues and feet. But the bull still did not stand firm, and God placed below it Behemoth, then water, then darkness: and that is as far as the human eye can see. In Hebrew myth, Behemoth is sometimes described as the deadly enemy of LEVIATHAN, who will slay and be slain by him at the Day of Judgement. (410, 444)

Bennu, *see* PHOENIX

Bergfolk In Scandinavian myth, these originated when the wicked angels were cast from heaven; not all of them reached hell together; some, namely the bergfolk, settled in mounds and banks, others, ellefolk or fairies, and BROWNIES or NISSE fell into mosses or into houses. Bergfolk were very small and sometimes identified with nisse. They could make themselves invisible and change their shape on demand. There was a tendency among them to steal corn and ale and other foods, they would borrow clothing, but for any favour done to them there would be a just reward. They rode three-legged horses, and were known to help in battles, but could only fire when a Christian had first done so. With their long noses they stirred the morning porridge in the pot. They are not unlike TROLLS in their habitat. (427)

Bhainsaura A buffalo-headed monster of Hindu mythology, which lived in the fields and would trample the corn harvest unless appeased by an offering of a pig, or unless worshipped when the rice was ripening. (470)

Bialozar, *see* KREUTZET

Biasd Na Srogaig Closely resembling a UNICORN, it lived only in small lochs on the Isle of Skye, and was a vast ungainly creature with immensely long legs. Its name means 'the beast of the lowering horn'. (509)

Bicorne An animal which ate only hen-pecked husbands. As these were so common, she was sleek and fat, and her panther's body looked more like that of a prize cow; she wore a broad grin, in contrast to the doleful look of her partner CHICHEVACHE. The two beasts were also known as *Bulchin* and *Thingut* in the sixteenth century.

Billdad   The Billdad was about the size of a beaver with long kangaroo-like hind-legs, webbed feet and heavy hawk-like bill. It lived off a diet of fish which it caught by lying in wait in the reeds; when a trout rose to the surface the billdad leapt with immense rapidity just beyond the fish, bringing its flat tail down with a resounding slap and stunning the fish, which it then picked up. A fully matured billdad could leap sixty yards. Found in North American lumberjack stories: see FEARSOME CRITTERS.   (412)

Bishop Fish   These curious fish emphasise a medieval tradition that everything in the air or on the earth had a double in the sea. The bishop fish had a mitred head, a scaly body, with two claw-like fins in the place of arms, and a fin-like cloak. Its legs appeared to be clad in rubber waders. Its origin was possibly the cast-up body of a giant squid. See also JENNY HANIVER, MONKFISH.   (308, 301, 422)

Bjära, *see* PARA

Blatant Beast, *see* QUESTING BEAST

Blemyae According to Pliny and medieval writers, they were an Indian race of creatures with no heads, their eyes and mouths appearing in their breasts. They were six foot high, and the entire body was gleaming gold with long beads covering their lower parts. (118)

Bloody Bones *see* RAWHEAD

Blue Men of Minch These were mermen of a very local kind, found nowhere except in the strait between Long Island and Shiant Island in the Hebrides. They were blue from head to toe. They were particularly affected by the spoken word; they could be bamboozled if addressed in rhymes, and no man needed to fear them if he could have the last word. They were particularly known for their power to conjure storms; when they slept the weather was fine. A local tradition held that they were fallen angels. (413)

Bodach, Bugbear or **Bug-a-Boo** A small but nasty creature which came down the chimney and snatched away children who had been naughty. Much beloved by nannies who ruled their wards with a rod of iron. (413)

Bogey Beast A general name for BOGGARTS, GRANTS and their ilk.

Boggart A mischievous spirit of the brownie type found in the North Country, particularly in Yorkshire. A favourite occupation of these creatures was to indulge in poltergeist activities. They are usually described as small, basically human creatures, but with animal traits such as fur or tails. A common story tells how a family plagued by a boggart decided to move house. When their chattels were loaded on a cart, a neighbour came up and said: 'So you're moving?' And the boggart answered from the back of the cart: 'Aye, we're moving.' (413)

Bogle Scottish version of the BOGGART.

Bonnacon (Bonachus, Bonasus) An Asian creature with a bull's head and horse's body which was covered in long mane-like hair. It had immense horns which curled round in multiple convolution to prevent it hurting people with the points; however, it was not devoid of protection,

since when it ran away it excreted in the face of its enemy. The excrement covered as much as three acres; any tree touched by it immediately caught fire and any hunter perished in flames.   (104, 118, 228)

Boobrie One of the shapes a WATER-HORSE could take. It was a vast bird shaped like a great northern diver but infinitely exaggerated, with white patches on its neck and breast. Its footprints covered the space of a pair of large antlers, and its voice was like the roar of an angry bull. This horrible monster haunted freshwater and sea lochs of Argyllshire, and made forays into the surrounding country where it devoured sheep and cows. See also WATER-HORSE.   (422, 508)

Boojum The lethal type of SNARK: quite unimaginable, and as delightful as it was unimaginable, except for those mortals who were unfortunate enough to meet one, their fate being to 'softly and suddenly vanish away'. The definition of a boojum has not progressed beyond that given in Lewis Carroll's sentimental fantasy *Sylvie and Bruno* by the Professor: 'once upon a time there was a Boojum; I forget the rest of the fable'. It is also the common name for a curious tree found in the Mexican desert.

Borametz, *see* VEGETABLE LAMB OF TARTARY

Borogove A wingless bird with a retroussé nose whose diet consisted exclusively of veal. Part of the fauna of Lewis Carroll's poem *Jabberwocky*.

Brash, *see* SHRIKER

Brazen Race These men, not born of women, played a part in the Greek concept of creation. They appeared on earth as though they had fallen as fruit from an ash tree and were already armed with brazen weapons. War gave them particular delight, but plague eventually erased them from the earth. See also TALOS.

Bread-and-Butter Fly This Looking-Glass Insect which Alice encountered on her adventures there had wings made of thin slices of bread and butter. Its body was a crust, its head a lump of sugar, and it lived off weak tea with cream in it.

Briareus, Gyes, Cottus The hundred-handed sons of Sky and Earth, with fifty heads, the hands symbolising the inlets of the Aegean.   (102)

Brollachan A shapeless thing found in tales of the Western Highlands of Scotland, responsible for many weird or inexplicable occurrences. (422)

Brownie Small shaggy creature of more or less human form, raggedly dressed, with hardly any nose. Found mainly in northern England and Scotland, although Cornwall too had its own brownies. They did odd jobs about the house, and the only payment they would accept was bread and milk. If a human tried to offer them more they would simply vanish. The Cornish brownies had a particular attribute in that they could make swarming bees settle.   (413)

Buccas Spirits found in Cornish mines, said to be spirits of Jews who once worked in the tin mines, and who were never allowed to rest because of their wicked slave-driving practices. They were the miners' friends, and knocked to warn them of impending disaster, and to point out good seams. Chinese miners told of a similar creature, the Celestial Stag, of uncertain shape, but with a human voice, which tried to bribe the miners to take it into the open air; if it did achieve its desire, it became a poisonous pool of liquid, while if the miner refused it could become troublesome and had to be walled up.   (411, 413)

Bucu, see KOORI

Bugbear or **Bug-a-boo,** see BODACH

Bulchin, see BICORNE

Bull of Inde Very large bull-like creature found in India. It had bright yellow hair which grew in contrary ways, and movable horns which could be put to any evil purpose. Its hide was so tough that nothing would penetrate it, and it was exceedingly cruel. If these bulls were caught they always killed themselves.   (119)

Bull, Winged Found in Persia and Assyria as early as the eighth century B.C., they were adopted for use in heraldic devices. The bull as a sacred symbol played an important part in the religion of this area, culminating in its role in the cult of Mithras.   (476)

Bunyip Found in Australian legend, it lived in deep pools or streams, and to satisfy its appetite it killed men; hence it was greatly feared by all natives. If a young bunyip was ever caught by a man its mother caused such a flood that everyone in the district was forced to retreat to a high hill. The flood, however, would not cease but would rise up the hill and touch their feet, whereupon they were instantly turned into black swans.

Since 1801, there have been persistent reports of an unknown furry water-animal, about the size of a dog, from various parts of Australia, perhaps based on stray seals. (487, 453)

Burach-Bhadi or **Wizard's Shackle** Eel or leech with nine eyes in its head and back, all of which squinted. Found in fords in the Western Highlands of Scotland, and also reported in Perthshire. It amused itself by entwining itself around the hooves of passing horses and drowning them so that it could then suck their blood. (509)

Busse A composite creature found in Scythia, with the head and horns of a hart, the body of a bull or cow, the colour of an ass. When hunted it changed colour like a man whose countenance changes when he is frightened. (321)

Bwbachod A Welsh brownie who was extremely friendly and industrious, who would work for anyone except teetotallers and dissenters, whom he despised. (413)

Cactus Cat The cactus cat lived in the great cactus district of Prescott and Theson in North and Central America. It had thorny hair; on the ears the thorns were of an exaggerated length and rigid. On its forearms above its front feet it had sharp knifelike blades of bone, and its tail was branched. It used the blades on its legs to slash the trunks of giant cactus plants, causing the sap to ooze out. This it did to a number of cactus plants systematically over several nights. By the time it had got back to the first plant the sap had fermented to form a sweet sickly substance

which the cat drank. It quickly became intoxicated and rushed off grating its bony excrescences together and uttering horrible shrieks. See also FEARSOME CRITTERS. (412)

Caecus Half-beast, half-man, he lived in a cave in the earth hidden from the sun. He slaughtered any man within his range, and arrayed the cave with their heads. He was thought to be son of Vulcan, from whom he inherited the ability to breathe fire. Hercules came across him on his return journey from Spain with Geryon's herd. Caecus gradually stole the cattle, dragging them backwards into the cave to disguise the direction they had gone. Eventually Hercules saw through this deception and slew the monster. (120)

Cailleach Bheur A giant hag in Scottish legend who symbolised winter. She could change her form when necessary to aid her deceits, either to that of a serpent or of a very beautiful maiden. She carried a staff which was captured by Spring, who flung it into holly bushes. No grass would ever grow where the staff fell. She was the patroness of deer and wild boar, and many hills including Ben Nevis and Schiehallion are associated with her.   (413)

Caladrius or **Charadrius** A white bird with a long swan-like neck and bright yellow beak and legs. This bird can identify fatal illness: if a man is going to die the bird turns his back on the patient, if the man is going to recover the bird takes the man's infirmity on itself, flies to the sun, vomits and disperses the sickness in the air. The dung of this bird was a cure for blindness. The caladrius was frequently found in the courts

of kings. In the later middle ages it became associated with jaundice, known as the court or royal disease, resulting from too much good living. The bird is frequently found in medieval ecclesiastical art, and it was closely associated with the Saviour Christ: the bestiary compares the bird to Our Lord, who will have nothing to do with those who are mortally sick in spirit. *Charadrius* is the generic name for plover in modern zoology.
                                                                    (432)

Callicantzari Callicantzari appear in modern Greek superstitions as two distinct species: a large grotesque race and a smaller, leprechaun-like type. The larger race could be as tall as a man or taller than two houses, but their features were always horribly distorted and enlarged, sometimes with goatlike elements. The smaller and less common type were mere hobgoblins, whose pranks were mischievous but not terrifying; they rode on animals as grotesque and deformed as themselves.

The larger callicantzari lived below the ground, where they spent their time trying to bring down the great tree which supported the world. Each year they almost completed their task, when the twelve days of Christmas came round and they were free to roam the face of the earth again; during these days the tree grew once more to its original size.

Even during their twelve days on earth, they could only appear at night; but they created havoc wherever they went, wrecking houses, carrying off women and forcing travellers to dance with them until exhausted. Occasionally they would even devour humans, but they could often be outwitted, and anyone who kept them at bay until cockcrow would see them vanish. They feared fire, and any home where the fire burnt brightly throughout the twelve days was safe from them.

On Chios, any child born during the twelve days of Christmas is regarded as particularly likely to become a callicantzaros, and must be branded on the heel to avoid this.

The derivation from the centaurs of classical myth is obscure, but has to do with the centaurs' skill in sorcery, and the survival of the centaurs' name after its precise meaning had been forgotten. (468)

Callitrice Resembling satyrs, they had beards and a broad tail on the rump and were found only in Ethiopia. It was not difficult to catch these creatures, who seem to have been relatively harmless. (118)

Calopus or **Chatloup** A wolf-like animal with curious horns whose projections and spikes frequently caused the animal to be irrevocably entangled in thickets. These creatures were found most frequently living by the river Euphrates. The calopus is occasionally found in heraldry. See also ANALOPOS, APTALEON. (312)

Calygreyhound   Like an antelope but with the fore-legs and claws of an eagle and the rear-legs and feet of an ox, it is sometimes compared in swiftness to a cheetah or wild cat. It appears in heraldic devices, and has been the badge of the de Veres, Earls of Oxford, since 1513.   (474)

Camelopard   A very graceful beast with the height and proportion of a camel but the skin of a pard. It is found on early Egyptian and Baby-lonian inscriptions, very frequently in pairs, where it does not appear to have any specific name. Its function in the realm of the gods is unknown, though it is depicted as a stellar god. It later featured in heraldic devices. The original camelopard was probably derived from a garbled account of a giraffe.   (490)

Camelopardel   Like the heraldic camelopard, except that it has two long horns which curve backwards.   (515)

Cametennus   An unspecified beast, similar to the METACOLLIN-ARUM.

Cantharus   A chaste fish-like creature. His greatest enemy is the adulterous SARGON. This fish is incredibly loyal to its mate and will fight to the death for her. He is the true emblem of faithful couples.   (321)

Capacti   A Mexican dragon from whose body earth was created. Cf. TIAMAT.

Capricorn   A goat-fish commemorated by Zeus in the constellation. Capricorn was created when Pan, among the other gods, was pursued by the demon Typhon; he leapt into the Nile before he had completely changed into a goat, his chosen form for escape, and became half-goat, half-fish.   (478)

Cat-Fish   A compound creature, part cat, part fish, found in heraldry; not to be confused with the ordinary catfish.

Cat-a-Mountain   Marco Polo describes in his famous account of his travels in the East a wild creature rather like a leopard with a great mouth, very keen eyesight and an attractive mien. It had a thin skin covering its

35

back and extending round the body to the feet. When it was still this remained gathered up, but when it hunted the skin stretched out and enabled it to fly from one tree to the next. The great speed it attained soon exhausted its prey which fell to the ground and was caught. Marco Polo's description seems to be inspired by flying squirrels or one of the larger bats, but later writers, including Shakespeare, used it as the ordinary name for any of the larger cats. (223)

Catoblepas According to Pliny, a small sluggish creature found in Ethiopia. Any man who beheld its eyes instantly fell dead upon the spot; however, the head of the catoblepas was so heavy that it was always bent

to the earth and its eyes were very rarely visible. Were it not for this, it could have proved the destruction of the human race. The name *Catoblepas* is now the generic term in zoology for the gnu. See also GORGON.

(118, 119)

Catoblepta Referred to by Sidney in his *Arcadia*: 'His impresser [device] was a catoblepta, which so long lies dead as the moone whereunto it has so natural a sympathy, wants her light.' Sidney is probably thinking of some other creature, and has named the catoblepas by mistake.

CENTAURS

Ccoa Evil cat spirit among Quechua Indians of Peru. It was about two feet long with a tail half that length marked with horizontal stripes. Its head was over-large in proportion to the rest of its body, and from its eyes and ears rained continual streams of hail. (470)

Celphie Curious Ethiopian beast which had man's hands for its five feet; its hind-legs from the ankle to the top of the calf were also human. The rest of its body was that of an animal similar to a cow. (119)

Cecrops In Greek myth, a son of Mother Earth, who, like ERICH-THONIUS, was part-man, part-serpent. He was the first king to recognise paternity, and he instituted monogamy.

Centaurs These are perhaps the most famous of the fauna of Greek mythology. They combined human and animal form, being most commonly human in front, merging with the body and hind-legs of a horse. They were the sons of Ixion and Juno in the form of a cloud, and lived in the Erymanthos range of mountains in Thessaly. The centaur was dignified and noble and was not associated with most other monstrous forms; the ancients looked upon the combination of human being and horse as a representation of good actions. The centaurs were certainly renowned for their benevolence, hospitality and wisdom. Cheiron was the most illustrious of them: famous for his knowledge of medicine, music and archery, he was Achilles' instructor. To escape everlasting agony inflicted by a poisoned arrow fired accidentally by Hercules, Cheiron surrendered his immortality to Prometheus. After this Zeus placed Cheiron among the stars, where to the Greeks he was represented by the constellation Sagittarius, the ninth sign of the Zodiac. The centaurs had one weakness in that they were very sensual; and they came to symbolise all forms of sensuality. When they became heated with wine they were liable to attack women, and this was the cause of the celebrated battle of the centaurs and the Lapiths. Eurytus, one of the centaurs, insulted the bride at the wedding of Pirithous and Hippodamia, to which many of the centaurs had been invited. A deadly battle ensued, and many centaurs were slain. It was at the end of this fight that Cheiron received his injury. Another well-known centaur was Nessus, who caused Hercules' death. The centaurs are also associated with the cloud horses of Vedic myths, known as GANDHARVAS. These had no riders, hence the idea of a rider so skilled that he became part of the horse. The centaurs are also reported to have made war on a weird Indian tribe of savages who had a horn in the middle of their head and lived in trees. They appeared in Christian iconography as a symbol of sensuality.

Pliny claimed to have seen an embalmed centaur, brought from Egypt in the time of Claudius; but this sounds suspiciously like a classical JENNY HANIVER. See also APOTHARNI. (433, 115)

Centycore A beast which had a hart's horn in the middle of its face, the breasts and thighs of a lion, large ears and mouth, and hooves like a horse; his muzzle was like a bear's, his eyes were very closely set, and his voice was like a man's. According to Solinus, the centycore is to be found in India. (206)

Cephus With the countenance of a satyr, in other respects it was a combination of a dog and a bear. It was bred in Ethiopia, and was worshipped by the Egyptians at Memphis. Strabo's account probably refers to an Egyptian deity, whose compound nature was symbolic rather than real. (120)

Cerastes or **Hornworm** A curious four-horned snake about a cubit in length and sandy coloured to blend with the surroundings of its desert habitat. It was found mainly in Africa. It appeared to be more flexible than most serpents and apparently had no spine. It lived off other creatures, both birds and beasts. To capture its prey the cerastes buried its body in the sand, leaving only its four horns exposed. With these it fashioned a little coronet in order to lure inquisitive animals, which it killed with its poisonous bite. *Cerastes* is now the generic name for the horned viper, a real snake with only two horns, but a very similar habitat.

Cerberus Dog with three heads each maned with serpents, guarding the gates of Hades' realm. Hercules' twelfth labour involved kidnapping Cerberus. Once he had achieved the task Hercules returned Cerberus, but not before the beast was exposed to sun and air. This had made the monster bark furiously; his slaver flew across the fields and gave birth to the poisonous plant named aconite. Cerberus can be compared to GARM, the dog of Hel in Scandinavian legend which barked at Odin when he went to consult the dead seeress Voha. (479)

Ce Sith A great dog as large as a bullock with a dark green coat which haunted parts of the highlands in Scotland. (413)

Cetus Sea monster with the body of a dolphin, a forked tail and a greyhound's head; it was not unlike a whale, but was fierce and carnivorous. Cetus was created by Jupiter to punish Cassiopeia for her vanity; it demanded her daughter Andromeda as reward for ceasing its ravages, and would have devoured her if it had not been for Perseus, who turned the monster to stone by producing Medusa's head. Cetus became a constellation in the Southern hemisphere, where it gazes at Andromeda from afar. (479)

Chac or **Tlaloc** American Indian rain god, whose head was represented as two intertwined serpents. Tlaloc was associated particularly with the top of mountains, where he had a special heaven for warriors who had fallen in battle and women who had died in childbirth. As water-god, he presided over the souls of the drowned, and as rain god he symbolised fertility, and maize belonged to him. (436)

Chamrosh Mythical bird of Iranian legend, sometimes confused with the SIMURGH. The chamrosh nested on the summit of Mount Elburz and protected Iran from invasion. Each year it gathered the seeds of all wild plants shaken by the simurgh from its tree and, mixing them with the rain, spread them on the earth. (208)

Chapalu Originally Palug's Cat, a magical creature slain by Cai in Welsh legend, the chapalu or capalus was later associated with the Mont du Chat in Savoy, where Arthur was said to have slain it, and appears in several Arthurian romances. The surviving fragments of the Welsh poem do not describe the cat, except to say that 'nine score fierce ones were its food'; in later stories it is simply a gigantic cat-monster. (475)

Charadrius, see CALADRIUS

Charun In Etruscan myth, the god of death and torment, an animal-headed man with tusks and flaming eyes; he delighted in his victim's agonies. The Greek ferryman of Hades, Charon, shared his name but not his character.

Chatloup, *see* CALOPUS

Cherubim Angels of light, probably adapted from Egyptian art, particularly from the form of Neth, the goddess of the heavens. There were four of them around the throne of heaven, one like a man, one like a lion, one like an eagle, one like an ox, and each one had six wings, all of which were full of eyes, and they sang constantly 'Holy, Holy, Holy, Lord God Almighty who was and is and is to come . . .' (Revelations, xlvi). (514)

Cherruve In South American Indian mythology, these minor deities, senders of shooting stars, are portrayed as man-headed serpents. (489)

Cheshire Cat Encountered by Alice in Wonderland. It had very long claws and a great many teeth, and the disconcerting habit of vanishing bit by bit, so that only its enormous grin remained. The expression 'to grin like a Cheshire cat' goes back to the seventeenth century and has never been satisfactorily explained; one suggestion is that a local painter was in the habit of painting grinning lions on inn-signs, another that Cheshire cheeses were sold with cats' faces moulded on them, as was done at Bath in the early nineteenth century. (521)

Chesterbelloc In appearance somewhat like a pantomime horse, the Chesterbelloc – at least according to George Bernard Shaw – was a not entirely co-ordinated creature worked by two men: all that Belloc, the forelegs, and Chesterton, who followed after, had in common was the virtue of literary talent and the vice (abhorrent to G.B.S.) of addiction to the pleasures of the table. Otherwise, they were 'not the same sort of Christian, not the same sort of Pagan, not the same sort of Liberal, not the same sort of anything intellectual. And that is why the Chesterbelloc is an unnatural beast . . .' Its Utopia was an essentially light-hearted one, 'a great game played by a herd of Chesterbellocs', or 'an orgy of uproarious drunkards', as opposed to the honest and possible Shavian Utopia. (504)

Chichevache A lean beast with a human face and cow's body that devours only obedient wives. These are rarely to be found; hence his lean and hungry appearance. Its partner is BICORNE, and it is also known as Thingut.

Ch'i-Lin The Chinese unicorn, which before the death of the Yellow Emperor, Huang Ti, at the age of one hundred and eleven, had appeared with the FENG-HWANG (the Chinese phoenix) as evidence of the benignity of his reign. When Confucius was born, a ch'i-lin appeared and spat out a piece of jade on which was written: 'Son of the water crystal, you shall be an uncrowned king!' At his death, the same ch'i-lin was hunted and killed by the Prince of Lu. The ch'i or male unicorn (lin being the female) killed only the wicked; it appeared as a symbol of justice on the caps of high officials. (486)

Chimera A compound monster described by Homer as having the fore-part of a lion, the hind parts of a serpent, and the body of a goat in

the middle. This creature is occasionally shown with three heads, following Hesiod's description, one of a lion, one of a goat and one of a dragon; in the late Middle Ages the Chimera was sometimes depicted with the face of a beautiful maiden. It was the offspring of TYPHON and ECHIDNE, and passed its life wreaking havoc in Lydia, breathing fire on any living thing which came within its range. It was ultimately slain by Bellerophon mounted on the winged horse Pegasus. (115)

Circhos According to Olaus Magnus, this Scandinavian sea monster was partly black and partly red in colour; in his feet there were two cloven places serving to make three toes. His right foot was small, but his left was very large, with the result that he walked with a dragging limp. Because he was so unstable he only walked about in fine weather; in times of storm he clung to a rock like a leech. (316)

Cinnamolgus The cinnamon bird found in Arabia. It built its nest high up in the tallest trees out of twigs of cinnamon. These nests were highly valued by the natives, but extremely difficult to reach. The boughs of the trees were too fragile for men to climb, so they knocked them down with arrows loaded with lead, and then sold the precious debris as spice. (118)

Cir Sith A fairy hound found in the western Scottish isles. It was the size of a two-year-old cow, and green in colour. The cir sith had a long tail which was usually coiled on its back, sometimes 'plaited like the straw-rug of a pack-saddle'. It was kept as watchdog in the fairy knowe, but did occasionally run loose; at these times it could be very dangerous. It moved swiftly, making a noise like a galloping horse, leaving footprints a span wide. It trailed travellers, barked three times, and at the third it overtook its prey and pulled him down. (509)

Cockatrice, *see* BASILISK

Cock-Fish This had a cock's body and a fish's tail. It is found in heraldry, although an extremely unusual charge. (439)

Conopenii Monsters found in Persia, with asses' heads and horses' manes. They breathed fire from their mouths and nostrils. (408)

Corocotta, Crocotte or **Crocuta** Cross between a hyena and an Ethiopian lioness. It had a disconcerting characteristic of never moving its eyeballs but staring directly forward. It lacked gums or teeth but had instead a solid piece of bone which could not be blunted. The corocotta could imitate the voices of men and cattle, and lure them into dense thickets and devour them. The crocotte is described as a cross between a dog and a wolf, but is in all other respects the same. (119, 101, 323)

Cottus, *see* BRIAREUS

Cow of Warwick, Dun A monstrous cow which was reputed to have come from Shropshire in the tenth century, where she provided milk for local giants, who used the druid circle on Staple Hill as a cow-pen. The Dun Cow produced an endless supply of milk, but an old crone, doubting this, produced a sieve to try the cow. The cow was so incensed that her yield should be questioned that she broke loose and wandered into Warwickshire, where she was slain by Guy of Warwick on Dunsmore Heath. Sir Guy had already chalked up a considerable record for destroying monsters; a dragon in Northumberland, the Windsor boar, and two Danish giants which had come to England. (458)

Creatures of Odin Two ravens known as Huginn (thought) and Muninn (memory) sat on Odin's shoulder and told him all they saw or heard. They went out scouting at daybreak and returned with the day's events on their tongues in the evening. Odin also had his wolves or hounds, Geri (ravener) and Freki (glutton) and SLEIPNIR, his horse.

Crocotte, Crocuta, *see* COROCOTTA

Crom Crumh Chomnaill A Gogmagog type of monster (see GIANTS) with immensely long hind-legs, so that he was taller than trees and buildings. A ball of fire was from time to time ejected from his mouth. He particularly terrified the Irish. St Maccrid lured the monster into a weir and killed him by touching him with part of his own clothing, the great goodness of the saint conquering evil. (430)

Cuero South American giant octopus with claws on the end of its tentacles; its ears were covered with eyes, and could become large or small at will. It occasionally went ashore to bask in the sun, but the effect of its returning to the sea was to produce a violent gale. Its description corresponds quite closely to a giant squid. (489)

Curupira A bald one-eyed dwarf with huge ears and a hairy body, always seen riding on a pig. His feet were either turned backwards or were double. He was found mainly in Brazil, where he was a Pan-like deity and very benevolent, although he insisted on certain stipulations being adhered to: for example, animals which were hunted had to be killed and not wounded. He would find lost cattle in return for the gift of tobacco. He was quite distinct from the *pe de garaffa* or bottle-foot of the Brazilian forest, whose strange tracks have not been satisfactorily explained by zoologists. (453, 489)

Cuter-cuss, *see* GUYASCUTUS

Cyclops The Cyclops were originally the powers of the air, Brontes (thunder), Steropes (lightning), and Arges (thunderbolt), who were the sons of sky and earth, bound and banished to Tartarus. In the Odyssey they appear as monsters with one eye in the centre of their forehead, living in caves; they fed on anything growing on their island (perhaps Nisida, off the Italian coast) including the flocks. Ulysses came up against Polyphemus, the greatest of all the Cyclops, on his journeys. He was captured but managed to escape by blinding the monster after making him drunk with wine. (102, 109, 111)

Cynamolgi Sir John Mandeville encountered this tribe of ferocious men with dogs' heads living around the source of the Niger, according to the spurious account of his travels. They wore the skins of wild animals and only conversed in barks. (219)

Cynocephali A tribe found in the East Indies which had hogs' teeth growing from their snouts, and as many again from behind their ears, according to Robert Burton's *Miracles of Art and Nature* (1676). They belonged, however, to art rather than nature. (306)

Cynocephalus   In the ninth century a monk at Corbie in Normandy, Ratramnus, was asked by his friend Rembertus whether these dogheaded men were to be regarded as men or animals. Ratramnus, relying on their knowledge of agriculture and their social habits, together with the human sense of their nakedness, declared them human despite the fact they did not talk but only barked communication. It is very likely that these creatures were baboons, about which the Greeks had dimly learnt. They had been one of the sacred beasts of Egypt, where they appeared in hieroglyphics, with a variety of meanings symbolising, for example, the moon, the habitable world, or a priest. The cynocephalus was reputed to die in parts, one part each day for seventy-two days. Some were acquainted with writing. At the equinoxes they uttered cries twelve times a day, once each hour. On no account would they eat fish.   (112, 461)

Dadhikra or **Dadhikravan**   Winged horse, swift as an eagle, representing the sun in early Hindu myth: there are also other horses in the same mythology which draw the sun god's chariot, including Etasa. Cf. ARRAK and ALSVID, in Scandinavian myth, and HORSES OF THE SUN.
                (484)

Daoine Sidhe   Heroic Irish fairies which partake of human nature, said by some to be fallen angels too good for hell. They have a penchant for beautiful mortals whom they steal for brides.   (413)

Delphyne   In Greek mythology, a serpent-tailed sister-monster of TYPHON, which guarded Zeus when trapped by Typhon.

Derceto, *see* ATARGATIS

Devil Biblical symbol of the ultimate all-powerful evil spirit, normally depicted as a horned creature carrying a three-pronged staff – often having six paws, a man's head and asses' ears.

Devil's Dandy Dogs A pack of fire-breathing black hounds found in Cornwall. They had livid fiery eyes, and followed the devil over lonely moors on stormy nights. If they captured humans they tore them apart limb by limb. The only known way to deter these monsters was for a man to pray sincerely. (413)

Devil Fish The fabulous version of this creature, compounded of the devil with a fish body, appears in heraldic devices: not to be confused with the real devil fish or manta ray. (476)

Dies A creature whose life-span extended from the rising of the sun to its setting. (458)

Direach Ghlinn Eitidh This one-handed, one-eyed and one-legged creature was a ghoul found in the west Scottish highlands, and is similar to the desert creature recorded by Marco Polo, otherwise known as a NESNAS. (222, 413)

Divis Devils of Persian myth, shown as cat-headed men with horns and hooves; they were originally the 'false' gods belonging to an earlier religion, the name deriving from the Vedic *deva* = gods. The same root-word produced both 'divine' and 'devil'. (448)

Dobie One of the BROWNIE clan, with clownish tendencies, he was the guardian of hidden treasure. Found most commonly in Yorkshire, he was sometimes taken for a ghost. (413)

Dog, Black The size of a young calf, with a long black shaggy coat and brilliant fiery eyes, it was quite harmless if left alone; but if a human spoke to a black dog or attempted to touch it he instantly became dumb and died. They appear in English fairy tales. (413)

Dogs, Sea Found in heraldry, these have the body of a talbot, but are covered in scales over their body; they have a broad scaly tail, and webbed feet. (439)

Donn of Cuálgne (Cooley)   A great supernatural bull described in the Irish poem *The Cattle Raid of Cooley*: he was especially renowned for 'the fifty youths who engaged in games, on his fine back finding room every evening to play draughts and engage in riotous dancing', by 'the hundred warriors he screened from heat and cold under his shadow and shelter . . . no sprite or goblin of the glen dared to come into one and the same cantred with him'. 'His musical lowing every evening as he returned to his shed and byre . . . was music enough and delight enough for a man in the north and south and in the west and in the middle of the cantred of Cooley.' His lowing alone was enough to put all the cows in calf.   (470)

Draci   Evil water spirits who preyed on women. They lured their victim by assuming the shape of a wooden plate floating on the stream. When the woman reached out to grab it, the dracus resumed his demon form and dragged her down to the bottom of the stream to nurse his children. Gervase of Tilbury related this particular story in the twelfth century in his *Otia Imperialia* or *Notes from the Imperial Court*.   (211)

Draconcopedes   In medieval myth serpents with women's faces, one of which is reported to have tempted Eve with the fatal apple in the garden of Eden.   (312)

Dragon   Among the oldest of mythological creatures, dragons appear in the traditions of virtually all peoples back to the beginning of time. Because of this widespread adoption the dragon appears in numerous forms, and local traditions have been created around many of them, crediting this tribe of monsters with many attributes. In their earliest form dragons were associated with the Great Mother, the water god and the warrior sun god; in these capacities they had the power to be both beneficent and destructive and were all-powerful creatures in the universe. Because of these qualities dragons assumed the roles taken by Osiris and Set in Egyptian mythology.

The dragon's form arose from his particular power of control over the waters of the earth and gave rise to many of the attributes singled out by different peoples as the whole myth developed. They were believed to live at the bottom of the sea, where they guarded vast treasure hoards, very frequently of pearls; rain clouds and thunder and lightning were believed to be the dragon's breath, hence the fire-breathing monster. The significance of the dragon was its control over the destiny of mankind. As the myth developed in the western world dragons came to represent the chaos of original matter with the result that with man's awakening conscience a struggle arose, and the created order constantly challenged the dragon's power. This type of dragon was considered by many to be the intermediate stage between a demon and the Devil and as such came into Christian belief. However, in the Eastern world the dragon adopted a rather different significance; he was essentially benevolent, a son of heaven, and controlled the watery elements of the universe. These dragons were the companions of kings, and particularly guarded royal treasures.

The Western type of dragon has been variously described, and individual dragons had their own unique forms. They appeared to be created from parts of various creatures, with the result that in general they were described as having eagle's feet and wings, lion's forelimbs and head, fish's scales, antelope's horns and a serpentine form of trunk and tail, which occasionally extended to the head. In colour they vary enormously; some are black, some red as in the Welsh version, some are yellow, and some Saxon dragons are white. In parts of Africa where the dragon is also considered as an evil power, the monster was believed to be the result of the unnatural union of an eagle and a she-wolf, and to have treble rows of teeth on both jaws (cf MANTICHORA). Some dragons had no feet but wings, some had neither feet nor wings. This latter variety were frequently confused with serpents. The destructive powers of the dragon derive from its fiery breath, which can devastate whole countries. Dragon's eyes also have this fiery red quality, sometimes believed to reflect the treasures they guarded; later traditions believed that misers would assume the form of dragons by constantly gloating over their treasure. The northern dragon, particularly in Scandinavia, sometimes assumed the form of a swan, swans symbolising excessive cold. It was thought by many that the dragon's form was symbolic of the most extreme physical conditions found in specific parts of the world. The dragon fears nothing except the elephant with whom he will engage in battle, entwining himself around the elephant and inflicting fatal blows. However, as the elephant finally collapses, his fall crushes the dragon to death. (In Arab countries, once a dragon had been captured, it was thought that to eat its heart and liver would endow men with the ability to understand the language of animals.)

The dragon is the enemy of the sun and the moon both in Eastern and Western mythology, and is believed to be responsible for eclipses. These occur when the dragon is attempting to swallow either of the heavenly bodies; which accounts for the dragon's appearance in primitive astronomy. In Armenian traditions, however, the fire and lightning god had powers to stay the dragon's control of the heavens, as could thunderbolts in Macedonian myth. A quite general belief was the dragon's association with death. A dead man was thought to become a dragon, while dragons were believed to be the guardians of treasures in burial chambers; cf. FAFNIR. Anglo-Saxon burial mounds which held treasure became known as the 'Hills of the Dragon'. Dragons' teeth, if planted, would grow into an army of men, a strange association with reincarnation. In the Greek legend of Cadmus his army was decimated by a serpent; he slew the monster and on Athene's orders planted the teeth, whereupon a host of armed men, the Sparti, sprang up.

The dragon occurs in the Bible, but is frequently confused with a serpent, and as such became identified with the serpent of Eden. In Revelation the battle between St Michael and the dragon, and the dragon's expulsion from heaven are related. The creature is described thus: 'And the great dragon was thrown down, that ancient serpent that was called the Devil. . . . And I saw the beast rising out of the sea with ten horns and seven heads, with ten diadems upon its horns and a blasphemous name upon its heads. And the beast that I saw was like a leopard, its feet were like a bear's and its mouth was like a lion's mouth.' Revelation (xii, 9, xiii, 1–2).

Because the dragon was the natural enemy of man, his death became the ultimate goal; consequently there are innumerable battles between gods and dragons, saints and dragons, and, in the medieval world, knights and dragons. In Egyptian mythology there is the conflict between Horus and Typhon, in Babylonia the Chaldean Tiamat was overcome by Marduk, in Greek legends the dragon fought on the side of the Titans and attacked Athene, who flung him into the heavens, where he became a constellation around the Pole Star; Hercules encountered and killed the dragon Ladon while fulfilling his eleventh labour. In Scandinavian literature Beowulf was slain by a dragon. The number of saints who encountered dragons is endless, St George being the most famous. St George reputedly had three

DRAGON

marks on his body, one being a dragon on his chest. After successful battles against the Saracens he went to Libya where a dragon was living in a lake near the town of Sylene. This dragon demanded to be fed daily with a virgin. When St George arrived the king's daughter Sabra was to be sacrificed; he gallantly offered to fight the dragon, wounded it, and attached it to the maiden's girdle who led it to the city to receive its dues from the citizens. The exact reason for St George being adopted as the patron saint of England is obscure. Other saints who encountered dragons include St Keyne, St Cado, St Guthlac and St Martha. This act in Christian terms symbolised the triumph of Christ over evil. The symbolism associated with the dragon appealed particularly to the medieval world; the monsters appear in various forms of Christian art, for instance entwined in sculptural forms in Celtic art. In medieval alchemy the dragon was the symbol of mercury and subsequently came to be used as the alchemist's sign.

In other terms the dragon symbolised power and was early adopted as a warlike emblem. As such the form was used in both East and West, adopted by the Emperors, and by the Romans as the emblem of a cohort; in the Celtic world the name came to mean chief, hence Pendragon. The Vikings called their warships dragon-barks. The Saxons used the dragon for their royal standard, and the Welsh dragon was derived from this by Geoffrey of Monmouth, although not actually used by the Welsh until Owen Glendower. The word dragon associated with fighting men survives in dragoniers and dragoons, who were men armed with dragons, i.e. short muskets which spout fire like the fabulous beast.

The dragon became associated with chivalry and romance, and tales of knights' feats in emulating St George and gaining a fair lady abound. It became a great honour to slay a dragon, and until this feat was achieved a knight could not be considered of the first rank: indeed, dragons almost seem to exist simply so that a hero can kill them. In England knights who achieved fame against dragons include Guy of Warwick, Sir John Conyers and Moore of Warncliffe. The last agreed to fight the dragon of Wantley (i.e. Wharncliffe) which had plagued herds of cattle and eaten three children. In return for his feat Moore demanded

'a fair maid of sixteen thats brisk,
and smiles about the mouth:
her hair as black as sloe.'

50

The ballad of *The Dragon of Wantley* goes on to describe the creature thus:

> *'This dragon had two furious wings one upon each shoulder,*
> *With a sting in his tail as long as a flail,*
> *Which made him bolder and bolder;*
> *He had long claws,*
> *And in his jaws,*
> *Four and fifty teeth of iron,*
> *With a hide as tough*
> *As any buff,*
> *Which did him round inviron.'*

The Chinese dragon (*lung*, in Japanese, *rin*) is essentially a benevolent dragon identified with the son of heaven. He has the horns of a stag, the head of a camel, the eyes of a demon, the neck of a snake, the belly of a clam, the scales of carp, the claws of an eagle, the pads of a tiger, the ears of a bull and long whiskers on his face, according to the philosopher Wang Fu. In his claw he grasps the staff Po Shan without which he cannot rise into the air. However, there are numerous variations on these features. There are dragons who control different elements: the four *lungs* are the guardians of the skies. The *t'ien lung* supports the mansions of the gods, the *shen lung* brings rain (the most characteristic association of Chinese dragons), and the *ti lung* controls rivers and streams. In the spring the *ti lung* was said to climb to the heavens, and the pressure of his feet on the clouds brought rain. In the autumn he took refuge in the sea. This dragon was sometimes known as the Blue Dragon and was similar to CHAC. The *fu-ts'ang lung* was the guardian of hidden treasure and of precious ores in the earth. The *li* controlled the seas, and the third type of dragon, the *kien*, controlled the marshes. The *kui lung* was hornless, the *ying lung* (in Japanese *hai ryo*) was winged and feathered. The Chinese dragon was closely associated with the Emperor, and the period of the Han dynasty was called the epoch of the fire dragons. These were sometimes known as dragon kings. Dragon kings occasionally had a separate identity, having human bodies with serpents on their crowns, and serpent retainers. They were the guardians of Buddha. The sea dragon kings were huge creatures a league long who lived in gorgeous palaces beneath the sea. Even Chinese dragons could try aerial tricks, but the Emperor's authority could usually control them, as in the case of the Emperor Yü, who when crossing a river found his boat being carried away by two yellow dragons. Everyone was afraid, but Yü laughed and said, 'I received my appointment from heaven, and labour with all my strength to benefit man. To be born is the course of nature; to die is heaven's decree. Why be troubled by dragons?' Hearing this the dragons curled up and slunk away. If ordinary people wanted to frighten a dragon, they made a great noise. The five-clawed dragon was the imperial symbol, especially in the Manchu dynasty. The Emperor Huang-ti, with seventy of his courtiers, was carried to heaven by dragons; and it became the custom when the Emperor died to say 'the dragon has ascended to heaven'. The Chinese dragon was particularly associated with chasing the sun in an attempt to bite it. In China there were many festivals and celebrations connected with dragons, who were thought to control the destiny of the people. Dragons appear to have been particularly fond of swallows. Anyone who had eaten a swallow was warned not to cross water in case the dragon there became jealous.

(440, 518)

The heraldic dragon has a huge body of reptilian nature covered with a mail of plates and scales and a row of formidable spines extending from head to tail, ending in a great and deadly sting. From gaping jaws with formidable fangs he belches flames. He has round luminous eyes, a dangerous spike on his nose, a forked tongue, eagle's feet and bat's wings. The dragon in heraldry is symbolic of power, wisdom and astuteness. The red dragon in heraldic terms was instituted by Henry VII from the supposed ensign of Cadwallader. The post of Rouge Dragon in the college of heralds is always filled by a Welshman. The red dragon of the Tudors indicated their Welsh ancestry. The arms of the City of London are supported by two dragons. See also DRAGON-TYGRE, DRAGON-WOLF.

See also DRAKES, FAFNIR, FIREDRAKE, GANDAREVA, GIRTA-BLILI, LUNG WANG, MUSHUSSU, SSU LING, TARASQUE, TIAMAT, VITRA, WYVERN.   (435, 436, 437, 440, 441, 511, 518, 521)

Dragon, Epidaurian Bred in Epidaurus, this dragon (unlike the usual Western dragon) was tame. He was a yellow-golden colour.

Dragon, Ethiopian An enormous monster reputed to be twenty cubits in length, sometimes having two, sometimes four, wings. This dragon was particularly renowned for killing elephants. It appears that there were four or five of them that lived on the Ethiopian coast; when nourishment was thin they twisted themselves together like so many osiers in a hurdle and set sail with their heads erect to find more food in Arabia. From the brain of the Ethiopian dragon came the stone called Dracontias, which had the power to make a house prosperous; however, it had to be taken from a living dragon. To do this involved drugging the animal with specially prepared grass before the operation could take place.

Dragon-Horse A compound creature which had the forepart of a horse and the huge lashing tail of a dragon. It was a vital spirit of heaven and earth and controlled rivers and lakes. It was worshipped as a rain god by American Indians. In Chinese mythology the dragon-horse was the messenger of heaven: a dragon-horse revealed to the Yellow Emperor the famous symbol of Yin and Yang, depicting the natural balance of the world between 'male' (active) and 'female' (passive) forces.

Dragon-Mermaid Found in Celtic myth, she gave favours particularly in the form of heirs to childless couples, but always demanded some sacrifice and laid a curse on the family if her wish was not fulfilled.

Dragon-Tygre A compound animal found in heraldic devices.

Dragon-Wolf Another compound animal found in heraldic devices.

Drakes In form these resemble the elaborate Indo-Chinese dragons; they are found in modern gypsy folk-tales of south-east Europe. The drake is an ogre with a human wife; he always travels on horseback and loves to hunt. His home is a glittering palace, but he will eat human flesh unless persuaded that the human visitor is a relation or can be helpful to him.

Dwarfs In Scandinavian myth dwarfs were little men, with large heads and usually with long beards, although some authorities prefer to regard them as beardless; occasionally they were covered with goose feathers or goatskins. They were born of mould and in the earth, like maggots, but the gods gave them human understanding, and they were consequently particularly wise on the subject of good and evil. They lived in hollow hills and cultivated the wasteland and scrub on the mountainside; this work had to be done at night because sunlight turned the dwarfs to stone. Dwarfs were particularly famed for their skill as smiths. It was they who taught men how to harden steel in water, and they themselves made weapons of special quality; often these weapons were endowed with magical powers. The dwarfs' magical powers all derived from their thin belts. If one of these was taken the dwarf would go to any extreme to retrieve it. The life-span of a dwarf exceeded all human age. There were four dwarfs who supported the four corners of heaven's domed arch.   (427, 480)

Ea or **Oannes** In Sumerian myth, the great giver of law and civilisation to the earth. He appeared from the sea in the times before the

Flood, when men had no laws and were like beasts. Ea spent his days among men instructing them in the ways of civilisation, but returned to the sea every night. He had a curious form, essentially like a fish, but below his fish's head he had a human head, and he also had human feet to enable him to move on land.

Eagle, Double-Headed   The two-headed eagle has its earliest prototype in Rome, symbolising supreme power. In stylised form it appears in Byzantine work. The double-headed eagle is found frequently in heraldry; it was the emblem of the Holy Roman Empire, and hence of the Habsburgs, and Prussia also used it.

Eale   The size of a hippopotamus with an elephant's tail and jaws like a wild boar, the eale was usually a black or tawny colour. He was found particularly in India, and was especially recognisable by his two curious horns, which were immensely long and were movable to give him added striking power when fighting. One useful feature of these horns was that the eale could roll one up when fighting to keep as a reserve if the other became blunted or broken. He was also equally at home in both the water and on dry land, so his enemies found it difficult to defeat him.   (118, 119)

Easg Saint or **Holy Fish**   These fish only inhabited wells near churches. There were usually two to a well; and they were regarded as sacred. They lived off hazel nuts which fell from the tree above the well. These nuts endowed the fish with magical properties, including oracular powers; to kill the fish would invite divine retribution. A pair of these fish were reported in a well near Kilmore Church in Lorne in the seventeenth century. They were said to have been there for centuries and were quite ageless.   (422)

Echidne   She was a beautiful woman to the waist, but below had the body of a man-eating serpent. Her lair was in a deep cavern. The results of Echidne's mating with TYPHON were various monstrous creatures of Greek myth, including ORTHOS, Geryon's watchdog, CERBERUS, the HYDRA, CHIMERA and the crafty serpent Ladon who guarded the apples of the Hesperides.

Ecidemon A beast so pure that even its scent would cause the most vile and poisonous creature to die. In Wolfram von Eschenbach's epic *Parzival*, this beast was chosen by Queen Secundille as a crest for Feirefiz to symbolise purity. Although described as snake-like, it was probably based on the ermine. (229, 506)

Eller Woman A very beautiful woman who would be absolutely perfect were it not for the fact that she had a hollow back, with the result that she looked like Henry Moore's interpretation of the female body. She was found particularly in Scandinavia. Like a MERMAID, she could seduce mortals and then reveal her own immortality. Cf. WOODWIVES. (413)

Elves Said to be descended from those of Eve's children whom she did not show to God because they were unwashed. God said, 'that which has been hid from me shall also be hid from men', which accounts for the fact that the elves were rarely seen. There were various kinds of elves: light elves, dark elves and black elves. The last were the same as dwarfs, but white elves are comparable in mythology to angels, less powerful than the gods but nevertheless very influential; they were more brilliant than the sun, and appeared in particular as white women in German legends. As mythology developed, elves became associated with small folk who lived underground, usually found wearing a hat or cap, very often red in colour. These elves loved music and dancing and practical jokes, and many mischievous tricks were performed by them. Today elf-rings and elf-mounds are still associated in country lore with these small people. (480, 413, 417, 427)

Empusae Greedily seductive female demons, having an ass's haunch, which symbolised lechery and cruelty, and each wearing one brazen sandal. They could change themselves from one form to another, including beautiful maidens, cows or bitches. Hecate was their mother; from her they inherited the brass sandal. The concept of the empusae appears to have reached Greek mythology from Palestine, and some authorities refer to them as spirits which particularly haunt the roads from Persia to India. (117)

Enfield A compound creature featuring in heraldry, particularly associated with some Irish families. It has the head of a fox, the chest of a greyhound, the body of a lion, the legs and tail of a wolf and the talons of an eagle, all forming a monstrous hound-like animal. (515)

Ephemerus, *see* BARNACLE GOOSE

Ercine These birds derived their name from the Hercynian Forest (now the Black Forest) in Germany. They were similar to a jay in every respect except that their feathers always appeared to be illuminated. The result was that however dark or dense the night they shed a phosphorescent light and thus guided travellers on their way. Sir Robert Chester describes them in his *Love's Martyr* (1601):

> *The gentle birds called the faire Hircinie*
> *Taking the name of that place where they breed,*
> *Within the night they shine so gloriously,*
> *That mans astonied senses they do feed;*
> *For in the darke being cast within the way*
> *Give light unto the man that goes astray.*

(228, 494)

Ereshkigal Queen of the underworld in Sumerian myth later equated or linked with Hecate. Her head had the form of a turban, and she had a snout-like nose. 'One horn, which is like that of a kid, on her back, is short. One horn, which is like that of a kid, on her forehead, is sharp. She has a sheep's ear and a human hand. With her two hands she carries food and holds it to her mouth. Her body is that of a fish and she is bent on her back. . . . From her loins to her soles she is a dog. . . . She is covered with scales like a serpent.' (106)

Erichthonius Serpent-tailed god of Greek legend, thought to be the father of Cecrops. Born of Mother Earth, he was nurtured by Athene, whose amorous adventures had led indirectly to his conception.

Erinnyes The three daughters of the union between air and Mother Earth featuring in one of the early creation myths. They were called Tisiphone, Alecto and Megaera, and also known as the three Furies. They punished crimes of parricide and perjury by relentlessly hounding the culprits from place to place. The Erinnyes were old crones, with snakes for hair, dogs' heads and coal-black bodies, bats' wings, blood-shot eyes, and in their hands they carried brass-studded scourges which caused their victims to die in torment. One of them has been described thus:

> *'A she-dragon of Hell, and all her head*
> *Agape with fangèd asps to bite me dead*
> *She hath no face but somewhere from her cloak*
> *Bloweth a wind of fire and bloody smoke.'*
> (Euripides, *Iphigenia in Tauris*, 285–9)

It was very ill-advised to mention the Erinnyes by name in conversation, hence they were frequently styled Eumenides, 'The Kindly Ones', to placate them. The third part of Aeschylus' trilogy the *Oresteia* bears this title, and deals with the Furies' pursuit of Orestes for killing his mother Clytemnestra.

Eros   The Greek God of Love, associated originally with the Orphic creation myth, but later symbol of a mystical doctrine of love. He was represented as double-sexed, golden-winged and having four heads; he sometimes roared like a bull or a lion, sometimes hissed like a serpent or bleated like a lamb.

Erymanthian Boar   An enormous beast which haunted the cypress groves of Mount Erymanthus and the thickets of Arcadian Mount Lampeia ravaging the countryside. The fourth labour of Hercules was to capture the creature alive, which he did by driving the boar into a deep snowdrift, where it got completely stuck.

Fachan   An evil and vicious Irish spirit, the bane of travellers. It had one hand protruding from its chest, one leg from its haunch, and one eye in its forehead like the Cyclops. Its whole body was covered with feathers, which had been contorted into strange shapes and appeared ruffled; on the crown of its head a tuft of these feathers stood up like a cock's comb. This demon pursued travellers, and leapt on them from behind, killing and mutilating them. (509)

Fafnir In Norse myth, one of the sons of Hreidmar, who with his brother slew his father out of greed for his golden treasure. Fafnir turned himself into a dragon and lay on the gold, only to be slain by the hero Sigurd (Wagner's Siegfried).

Falcon-Fish A compound creature found in heraldic devices, which besides its combined bird – fish features had hound's ears. (476)

Falin A Scottish mountain demon, haunting particularly Glen Aven. He had a head twice as large as his body, and inhabited the highest crags of the mountains. This was a dangerous spirit, having no natural form, and appearing very occasionally. He was only seen about the break of day, and any creature which crossed the track along which he had been before the sun had shone on it to dispel his evil was doomed to certain death. (509)

Fanesii A tribe of men found in the Southern Ocean and reported by Pliny to have ears that were so vast that they could cover their whole body with them. (118)

Fauns Attendants of PAN, these half-human creatures had goat's horns, and the lower part of their body was a goat's hindquarters. They were a male counterpart to nymphs and akin to satyrs, though usually portrayed as being younger.

Fearsome Critters The fabulous fauna of the American West derives from the humorous tales of the lumberjacks and other frontiersmen, whose chief amusement was the 'tall story'; these developed into a kind of cycle centred on the mythical Paul Bunyan. Some creatures such as the HOOP SNAKE and the GUYASCUTUS go back to the early nineteenth century, though many are more conscious inventions by later writers, often hilarious (see SQUONK), and salted with a little dry learning to heighten the effect. It is curious to find an occasional borrowing from much older legends among the fantasies, for instance that of the animal which sleeps standing up: compare the HODAG and the ACHLIS. The SHMOO is a modern descendant of the tradition, though more orthodox inventions such as the GLAWACKUS continue to be added. (412, 492, 470)

Feathered Men A tribe reported by Sir John Mandeville on his travels whose bodies were covered with feathers except for their faces and the palms of their hands. They could live both on land and in the sea. Their diet was of raw flesh and fish. (219)

Feng-Hwang (Japanese **Ho-o**) Although it is called the Chinese phoenix, the equation between feng-hwang and phoenix is not absolute. The feng-hwang is not unique: feng is the male bird, hwang the female.

But in other respects it resembles the Western phoenix. It is renowned for its sweet song, and is accompanied by crowds of birds. It is a heavenly emissary which appears when the land enjoys the gods' favour, and is not seen in warlike times, just as in Roman Egypt the phoenix was a good omen. It first appeared in the reign of Ch'eng Wang, who composed a song attributing its appearance entirely to the virtues remaining from the days of former kings, disclaiming those virtues himself. Before Huang Ti, the Yellow Emperor, died, the feng-hwang appeared with the ch'i-lin (unicorn) as evidence of the benevolence of his reign. The feng-hwang last appeared at the grave of Hung Wu in A.D. 1399. The problem of rarity is complicated by reports that when you play the flute, nine times out of ten the creature will appear to accompany you, and when friends gather in a garden in the cool of the evening to play music together it will often join them. The feng-hwang, however, is really part of the other world, as one of the four spiritual creatures, symbol of the empress and of the element fire. It bears on its body the characters for virtue, righteousness, humanity, sincerity and integrity; it will eat no living thing, not even grass; and of all four spiritual creatures, tortoise, ch'i-lin, dragon and feng-hwang, it is the feng-hwang which is the most exalted. See SSU LING. (463, 518, 486)

Fenris-wolf (Hrodvitnir) Offspring of the god Loki in Norse mythology. This wolf-child was fed by Tyr, the god of war, and grew immensely strong. The gods, fearing his power and remembering prophecies, took him and determined to bind him fast, but so mighty was his strength that they could find no fetter strong enough to hold him. The problem was solved by the dwarfs, who fashioned the fetter Gleipner out of a curious collection of materials, the noise of a cat's footfall, the hair of a woman's beard, the roots of a rock, the sinews of a bear, the breath of a fish and the spittle of a bird; all these supposedly non-existent things fashioned a magic cord. However, the wolf was suspicious and would only allow himself to be bound if one of the gods agreed to put his hand in the wolf's mouth. Tyr was the only god brave enough to volunteer; the monster was bound, but Tyr lost his hand. The Fenris-Wolf was bound to a rock, where he must remain until Ragnarök, or the doom of the gods. At Ragnarök the Fenris-Wolf will swallow Odin, but Vidar, Odin's son, will seize the wolf by the jaws, and setting his foot on the lower jaw with a great display of strength will tear them apart and slay the wolf. The sons of the Fenris-Wolf are said to pursue the sun and moon, and swallow them alternately, producing day and night. (438)

Fetch In English folklore of the fifteenth and sixteenth centuries, an evil demon who roamed about by day and night; only in the darkness could it exude its evil qualities, and anyone who saw it by night was certain to die imminently. Later, in the eighteenth century, the word came to mean a wraith or apparition of a living creature. (413)

Firedrake A type of cave-dwelling dragon which hoarded treasure, and breathed fire, closely associated with grave mounds to guard the treasure buried with the dead. It was believed by some that the dragon was the dead man's spirit, and the dragon came to symbolise triumph over death, appearing in carving on coffins. Fafnir is one example of these dragons, who are a particular feature of northern mythology. (470)

Flitterbick A type of American flying squirrel whose flight is so rapid that when it hit an ox between the eyes the blow was sufficient to kill. They are consequently very dangerous, and because they are so rapid it is impossible to take evasive action. See FEARSOME CRITTERS. (412)

Fomorians Hideously mis-shapen monsters of Celtic myth. Balor, the chief of them, had one good eye and one evil eye; it took four strong men to force open the lid of his good eye.

Formicoleon, *see* ANT-LION

Fox-Spirit An apparently human creature, who although physically killed could not be spiritually annihilated. One such fox-spirit, disguised as a beautiful maiden, became the wife of the Emperor Hansoku, who on her account murdered over a thousand men. Such fox-spirits, together with goblin-spirits, occurred frequently in Japanese tales. Often they had flames flickering over their heads, and after a thousand years they turned white or golden and mounted to heaven, having lost all their sin. In their spirit form they were masters of illusion, and were known to impersonate Buddhist priests. They were also reputed to be fire-raisers in the temples.

Once they had ascended to heaven they became associated with the rice-spirits and had control over the crops. In Chinese myth they played a similar part: they could possess men, and in this guise were particularly fond of chicken, and they could pursue a malignant feud with a family who had offended them. The fox-spirit was worshipped as 'Great Father Hu', but was only recently admitted as a divinity during the last century. These foxes were capable of making the elixir of life, which they breathed out as a ball of fire as they perfected it on moonlit nights; a cunning observer could seize it from them. They were the particular enemies of dragons, and protected themselves by carrying unclean objects which the dragon would not touch. (518, 519, 463)

Freki, *see* CREATURES OF ODIN

Fuath A water spirit, found in Scotland and of a malignant bent. It had webbed feet, yellow hair, a tail, mane, no nose, and was dressed in green. The name fuath has become a general term to describe any kind of nature spirit, but usually of the malignant species. (481)

Furies, *see* ERINNYES

Fylgja A Norse guardian spirit, usually in animal form, either an eagle, wolf or a troll. It appears especially in dreams as symbolic of a certain person; the qualities of the animal depicted correspond to the qualities of the person. Men who were approaching death saw their own fylgja; occasionally it appeared as the 'double' of its owner. Cf. FETCH.

Gabriel Ratchet A spirit hound which hunted high in the air. It could be heard yelping overhead in the midst of violent storms, and to hear these yelps was a presage of death. In the North of England it was thought that they might be the souls of unbaptised children. (413)

Galon   Indo-Chinese name for the GARUDA.

Ganapatihardiya, *see* GANESHA

Ganconer or **Gacanagh**   One of the host of little people: the ganconer's particular attribute was to beguile young girls by talking to them.
They fell so hopelessly in love with him that when he deserted them they
pined away and died for love of him. The Irish version of these little
people had a city of their own in the depths of a lough, from which they
emerged periodically to steal cattle.   (413)

Gandareva or **Kundrav**   In Sumerian myth, a monster fiend of the
depths, known as Master of the Abyss. It was dragon-like in form with its
body in the waters and its head in the sky. It was the guardian of an evil
dragon whose great desire was to destroy the world, and slew many men;
but he was eventually slain by Keresaspa after a gruelling battle of nine
days and nights. When Keresaspa first saw the monster it was in need of a
toothpick to extricate the dead men from its teeth. Although Keresaspa
flayed it constantly, the demon still survived and ate Keresaspa's fifteen
horses, blinded him, pushed him into a thicket and carried off his wife and
family. However, Keresaspa soon recovered and had his revenge, rescuing
his family and slaying the monster. A survival of the same legend, albeit in
much altered form, was Gandarva, the sun steed and measurer of space in
Vedic myth, who was sometimes identified with the rainbow. The
similarity of names has caused confusion with the GANDHARVAS.
                                                                  (470, 484)

Gandharva or **Kinnara**   The Indian equivalent of the centaurs, they
were shaggy half-animal beings, normally shown with the body of a horse
and head of a man, or less usually the other way round. They were the
lovers of the APSARAS and may have been the spirits of warriors killed in
battle.

Ganesha   A creature of Indian mythology, having a human body and
an elephant head. His body was rotund and red, and he had four hands, in
one of which he carried a rosary. His head was white, and he lacked one
tusk; it is reputed that in a fit of extreme anger he tore out one tusk and

hurled it at the moon, obliterating its light – hence the waxing and waning cycle of the moon. The ganesha rode on the back of a rat, formerly considered among the most powerful of demons. Originally he was probably a straightforward elephant god, but his head was later said to have resulted from a struggle between the gods, his original one being turned to ashes, and replaced by the first available one, which happened to be that of an elephant. The ganesha was renowned for his gluttony and laziness, but despite this, in moments of necessity, he was exceedingly strong and brave. In the Tantras, a female equivalent, Ganapatihardiya, appears. (470)

Gargouille A dragon which lived in the Seine, whose particular attribute was to make waterspouts. This dragon ravaged Rouen, and was slain by St Romans in the seventh century. Because of his habit of spouting water he gave his name to gargoyles.

Gargoyle Stylised medieval creature, frequently of animal derivation, although some gargoyles have human faces. Their common factor is an attenuated body and a wide open mouth. They are frequently found on medieval buildings, usually of a religious nature, as part of the drainage system of the roof. Water is channelled through the bodies of these creatures, which act as a pipe, and it gushes out of the mouth, and is thrown clear of the building to the ground.

Garm, *see* CERBERUS

Garuda Bird Bird of life, destroyer and creator of everything, the garuda is one of the most ancient figures in mythology. As time passed the garuda became identified with the standard of Vishna and his vāhana or vehicle, and acquired certain human attributes. He was the implacable foe of the snake demons or NĀGĀS, on whom he preyed with his six sons. In one episode, the garuda's mother, Vuiata, became the slave of a family of nāgas, and the garuda had to steal the dew of immortality from the gods in order to rescue her. In Buddhist mythology, when the nāgas came to hear Gotama Buddha preach, they had to be protected from the garudas, whom the Buddhists regarded as demons. The great strength and determination of the garudas resulted in their becoming the symbol of victory.

Yet despite this mighty power, they were in Indian mythology never cruel to humans. In Indonesian myth, however, the garuda was identified as a roc-like creature and did prey on men. (470, 484)

Gerahav According to the medieval bestiaries, a sea bird, which laid the most enormous eggs, produced with great pain. She hid the eggs in the depth of the ocean, and kept a close watch for fear of enemies. When the eggs were about to hatch, the bird rose to the surface until the chicks broke out of the shell; and then she dived down and led them to the shore to feed them. (204)

Geri, *see* CREATURES OF ODIN

Geryon The son of Chrysaor and Callirrhoë, Geryon was the King of Partessus in Spain and reputedly the strongest man alive at the time of Hercules' labours. He was born with three heads, six hands and three bodies joined together at the waist. He owned a herd of very beautiful red cattle. The tenth labour of Hercules involved the theft of these cattle which he successfully accomplished, shooting Geryon from the side through his three bodies. It is not clear whether Geryon died, but he lost his cattle, and from his blood a tree sprang up which when the Pleiades rose bore stoneless cherry-like fruit.   (442)

Ghul An evil spirit which appeared to travellers in the Arabian desert, by night. The traveller took it for a comrade and was led astray. It was sometimes compared with the EMPUSAE. Marco Polo quotes ghuls, along with the gryphon and good faith, as the three things which, though frequently referred to, exist nowhere. The name is the origin of our word 'ghoul'.   (222)

Ghul-I-Beában One particular ghul of monstrous size found in Afghanistan and Persia and known as the goblin of the wilderness. In the manner of a ghul, it attacked and devoured strangers.   (222)

Giants The idea of a gigantic, monstrous race who were responsible for the physical aspect of the world is common to many mythologies. The Chinese spoke of P'AN KU, whose body became various parts of the earth when he died, while the Greeks saw the giants as the spirits of untamed creation. They were said to have been born when drops of Uranos' blood fell onto the earth from the wound inflicted on him by his son Kronos. As Kronos was the father of the gods, it was scarcely surprising that gods and giants should wage war on each other. The giants made three attempts to overthrow the gods, the first being a general assault, at the end of which some of these monstrous serpent-footed creatures were buried under islands. But Gaia, Uranos' consort, produced one more monster, TYPHON, who was again buried by Zeus, this time under Etna. The ALOADS were the third and last power to attempt to overthrow the gods, but their story is a later addition; unconnected with the struggle between Zeus and the earth-giants, they seem originally to have been deities from Asia Minor.

GIANTS

In Scandinavian myth, the giants belonged to the very earliest moments of creation. Between Muspill, the land of fire, and the land of snow and ice there lay the desert Ginnungagap, where the first living being, the giant Ymir, arose.

It was Time's morning
When Ymir lived;
There was no sand, no sea,
Nor cooling billows.

Earth there was none,
No lofty heaven,
No spot of living green,
Only a deep profound.

From Ymir came the human race and the frost giants. From another being who arose in the desert were descended the three gods Odin, Vili and Ve. These three slew Ymir, and used his body to create the world: his body made the earth, his blood the sea, his hair the trees, his skull the heavens, his brain the clouds, and his eyebrows Midgard, where the human race was to dwell. All the frost giants save Bergelmir were drowned in Ymir's blood; from him were descended the giants who dwelt in Jotunheim, rivals of the gods but unable to match their power.

The giants of Celtic and modern European folklore are altogether more mundane creatures. They were regarded as men of abnormal size, strength and appetite, but with little brain. Occasionally they could be benevolent, but they also appeared as ogres, ferocious creatures living off human flesh. Many stones, caves and other natural features were attributed to them, the most famous being the Giant's Causeway in Northern Ireland, reputedly fashioned by Fingal, the denizen of Fingal's Cave.

English giants were believed by some to have sprung from the thirty-three infamous daughters of the Emperor Diocletian. They murdered their husbands, and were set adrift in a ship which eventually reached Albion. There they fell in with some demons, and their offspring were the 'few giants' who, according to Geoffrey of Monmouth, were the only inhabitants of the island when Brutus arrived from Troy. Geoffrey himself does not offer any explanation of the giants' origin, but describes how the last of them was eliminated from the island. Corineus of Cornwall particularly enjoyed wrestling with the giants, and when Brutus was attacked by a horde of them at Totnes, he slew them all except for a monster called Gogmagog, 'who was twelve feet tall. He was so strong that, once he had given it a shake, he could tear up an oak-tree as though it were a hazel wand.' This creature he offered to Corineus as a wrestling-partner: 'The contest began. Corineus moved in, so did the giant; each of them caught the other in a hold by twining his arms round him, and the air vibrated with their panting breath. Gogmagog gripped Corineus with all his might and broke three of his ribs, two on the right side and one on the left. Corineus then summoned all his strength, for he was infuriated by what had happened. He heaved Gogmagog up on to his shoulders, and running as fast as he could under the weight, he hurried off to the nearby coast. He clambered up to the top of a mighty cliff, shook himself free and hurled this deadly monster, whom he was carrying on his shoulders, far out into the sea. The giant fell on to a sharp reef of rocks, where he was dashed into a thousand fragments and stained the waters with his blood. The place took its name from the fact that the giant was hurled down there and it is called Gogmagog's Leap to this day.'   (210)

A later version separates Gog and Magog into two separate creatures, who became the porters at Brutus's palace in London. The name itself is Biblical (Ezekiel xxxviii 1); Gog was the prince of Meshech and Tubal, and Magog his original home.

The figure of Gogmagog has innumerable parallels in other mythologies and literatures; most of these derive from corrupt retellings of the stories in which giants appeared as spirits of untamed nature, but the substance of such tales was made much more credible by rare cases of gigantism in real life and by the discovery of the fossil remains of prehistoric creatures. Medieval knowledge of anatomy was slight, and any such find from a beast of uncommon size was immediately classified as giants' bones.   (210, 438, 498, 501)

Giant Ants, *see* ANTS, ETHIOPIAN

Giant Mice, *see* MICE, GIANT

Giddyfish   Small very elastic fish like india-rubber, which were caught through holes in the ice in the winter by hitting one on the head with a paddle. This fish would bounce up and down, and all the others would copy it until they had all bounced through the hole in the ice and could just be picked up on the surface. Found in North American folk-tales. See FEARSOME CRITTERS. (412)

Gigelorum or **Giol-Daoram** The most microscopic of all creatures, it nested in a mite's ear, and could never be seen by the naked eye. Found in Scotland. (413)

Gillygaloo A bird whose habitat was hilly land. She laid square eggs so that they would not roll down the hill. Lumberjacks in North America hardboiled these eggs and used them for dice. See FEARSOME CRITTERS. (412)

Girtablili Half-man, half-scorpion, this creature appears as one of the dragons of Tiamat in the Babylonian epic of creation.

Glas Gaibleanir Literally translated, this means the grey white-loined cow. Found particularly in Scotland, she often stayed with poor families to assist them until a fool struck her, or she was milked into a leaky bucket (see COW OF WARWICK, DUN) when she would depart. Where she slept there was always abundant grass. A saying has evolved around this: 'The grey cow slept there', meaning that the particular piece of land referred to is a very fertile field. (470)

Glastig A Scottish highland spirit, half-woman, half-goat in form, and clothed in green. This creature had a bit of all the fairy attributes in her, but was particularly kind to old people and the feeble-minded. She worked in the house and did many useful things, but did, however, have her wicked side which came out in a habit of waylaying travellers and mis-directing them. Like a Kelpie, she was also partly a water spirit and could be caught and set to work. (413)

Glawackus An American beast variously described as resembling a lion, a cougar, a panther or a boar. It was seen in Glastonbury, Connecticut, in 1939, and again in November 1944 at Frizzleburg, Ma., where it fought with a bull: probably a local journalist's continuation of the FEARSOME CRITTERS tradition. (492)

Glooscap Another name for MANABOZHO.

Goat, Sea This Sumerian goat that lived in the water provided transport for Ea or Marduk, who stood on the creature's back. The Indian sea goat is related to the MAKARA. (483)

Gollinkambi, *see* VITHAFNIR

Goofang This curious fish always swam backwards in order to keep the water out of its eyes. Found in North American folk tales, *see* FEARSOME CRITTERS. For a European parallel compare ACIPENSER. (412)

Goofus A curious bird found in North America and recorded by lumberjacks. It flies backward, because, so it is said, its only interest is in the places it has visited. It also builds its nest upside down, though how it uses this nest is not explained. See FEARSOME CRITTERS. (412)

Gorgon In Greek mythology there were three Gorgons, Stheino, Euryale and Medusa, originally all very beautiful maidens. Medusa, because she slept one night with Poseidon, was changed by Athene into a winged monster with glaring eyes, huge teeth, projecting tongue, brazen claws and serpent locks, and whose gaze turned men to stone. Perseus, with the help of Athene, slew Medusa by never looking directly at her, but only at her reflection in his shield. He cut off her head, and using it for protection (for Medusa's eyes still turned men to stone), took it to Seriphos, where he gave the head to Athene. The drops of blood that fell from it into the sea on the way became the scarlet coral branches called gorgonia.
    The story of the gorgon was much elaborated. She was frequently described either as a bird which looked like a proud woman, or as a very beautiful seductive woman with golden hair. She sometimes played and laughed, at others raged furiously around the mountains of the west, and when the day of her longing arrived she cried to all creatures, 'come to me and satisfy the desire of the flesh', but all who came to her died. It was thought she was only annihilated by an enchanter, who persuaded her to dig a hole near the river and lay her head inside, so that he should not see her; he then promised to go to her, which he did, but cut off her head

before seeing her face. Like Perseus, he kept the head as a protection against his enemies.

In the sixteenth century the gorgon was believed to be real, and was thought to come from Africa. It was fearsome to see, with thick eyelids, eyes like an ox, always bloodshot, a long hanging mane which fell from the crown of its head to the ground, concealing the eyes which always looked down. It had teeth like a swine, wings, hands, and was the size of a small bull. The whole of its body was scaled like a dragon. The gorgon lived off poisonous herbs, and breathed poisonous breath on its enemies, although the tradition of killing with its eyes was still upheld by some. Its heavy head was regarded as some curb to its powers, as it only ever looked up when it was provoked. This creature appears to have been the CATOBLEPAS, under another name. (102, 214, 204, 321, 322)

Graeae Three sisters in Greek mythology, named Enyo, Pemphredo and Deino. They had grey hair from birth, and only one eye and tooth between the three of them. They came to personify the terrors of the sea, and appeared as great billows in the open main. (417)

Grant An English demon in the form of a yearling colt which walked on its hind-legs and had fiery eyes. It was particularly a town spirit and either at midday or just after sunset it would run down the middle of the street. All the dogs emerged and barked furiously, and this was said to be a warning of imminent danger. Some people have seen a connection with Grendel. (413)

Gremlins First noted in the First World War by the Royal Naval Air Service, but not named until 1922, when an R.A.F. pilot called Le Bourget for a weather report and was told 'Gremlins sur la Manche', whereupon his radio died. The word was derived from Old English *gremian* – to vex. Vex they certainly did: the R.A.F. has countless tales of gremlin pranks. During the Second World War, they were to be found in literally every aircraft that came off the production line. They stood about twelve to twenty inches high, and appeared rather like a North American jack-rabbit which has been crossed with a bull terrier; they usually wore green breeches and a red jacket, always with spats and a top hat. (Some marine species had webbed feet and fins on their heels.) They had no wings, so they always travelled as passengers. When they were off air duty they lived in underground dwellings with rabbit-hole entrances on the periphery of airfields so that they could sneak on board unnoticed. One of their most pernicious habits was to drink petrol, their favourite beverage, but most embarrassing for the pilot. They sometimes travelled in contingents and could so upset the balance of a plane by rushing from one wing to the other, that the crew had to bale out. The gremlins then joined hands, expanded their large feet and parachuted gently to earth,

head downwards, their top hats absorbing the shock of landing. It was also well known that gremlins had succeeded in underpinning with large hydraulic jacks practically every training aerodrome in the country. The duty gremlin controlled these jacks and when a young pilot was just flattening out to land he yanked his lever and the whole airfield either sank ten feet or shot up ten feet, either result being equally disconcerting. The gremlins would go to any length to obstruct the navigator, even under extreme conditions shuffling all the stars in the heavens; they also inter-fered with the wireless, so that just before it packed up there would be a fiendish and chilling static howl, at which it was also advisable to examine all control wires.

They have now invaded almost all types of electronic and mechanical equipment, and are so widespread as to be taken for granted.   (445, 520)

Grendel   Grendel and his mother were believed to be descended from Cain and were regarded as foes of God, in the Anglo-Saxon poem *Beowulf*, which tells of the building of Heorot by the Danish King Hrothgar, and the attacks by Grendel, 'this gruesome prowler of the border land, ranger of the moors, the fen and the fastness', on his men. He always entered the hall at night, and swiftly wrought havoc there: 'At once the hellish mon-ster, grim and greedy, brutally cruel, started forward and seized thirty thanes even as they slept.' Beowulf, hearing of these attacks, offered his assistance, and lay in wait for Grendel. The monster was captured as he returned to his prey and 'Then time and again Beowulf's band brandished their ancestral swords' until 'fatally wounded, Grendel was obliged to make for the marshes leaving his arm in Beowulf's grasp'. Later, when searching out his mother Beowulf found Grendel on his deathbed, and cut off his head; it took four thanes to carry the trophy back.   (203)

Griffin, Gryphon, or **Griffeth**   Found in India and Arabia, this creature was part lion, part eagle, combining the qualities of the lion as king of the beasts and the eagle as king of the birds. It had four lion's legs with eagle's claws, which were enormously strong and could lift a man on horseback and carry him off. Its head and wings were those of an eagle. The back feathers were black, the front red, the wings white and the neck a deep blue. It was the largest of all birds, and when it spread its wings it intercepted the rays of the sun; hence it has become associated with the guardian of golden treasure. Some authorities say that only the female griffin is winged, but this is not generally held to be true. Huon of Bordeaux described it thus: 'His becke was marvaylously greate, his eyes as great as a basyn, and more redder than the mouthe of a fornays and his talantys so great and so longe that fearful it was to beholde hym.' Accord-ing to Herodotus, the griffins lived in high mountains in India, where they

74

dug up gold and built their nests of it; this gold was much coveted by men, but the griffins were tireless guardians and it was impossible to pass them. They also put agate in the nest for its medicinal value. Some say that the gold-bearing mountains also produced jasper and emeralds which the griffins guarded equally jealously. There were frequent fights between the griffins and the ARIMASPI, the one-eyed tribe of Scythia, over the gold.

The griffins' claws were also greatly prized, as they were reputed to change colour in the presence of poison. It was believed that only a holy man could acquire them, and then only if he had healed the griffin of some hurt. They preyed on dead men to provide nourishment for their young and themselves devoured horses, the animals they hated above all others.

The griffin has many symbolic aspects, in hieroglyphs he represents heat and summer, taken from his association with the sun. He is taken to symbolise both the divine and the human element in Christ. The griffin is also sacred to Apollo. The Middle Eastern griffin is basically harmless unless provoked, but the image of the griffin in Europe is of a rapacious beast much to be feared.

The griffin can be compared to the Russian Senmurv or Sumargh, to the GARUDA, to the SIMURGH in Oriental literature, kargas in Turkey, kirni in Japan, the ANGKA of the Arabs and the BAR YACHRE, and also to the heliodromos (see PHOENIX).   (214, 109, 116, 101)

Griffin Vulture Born of TYPHON and ECHIDNE in Greek mythology, this bird pecked at Prometheus' liver for thirty years. Hercules freed Prometheus from this torture by shooting the griffin-vulture with an arrow. It has given its name to the modern griffon vulture (*Gryps fulvus*).

Gryphon, *see* GRIFFIN

Grouse, Pinnacle This North American bird had only one wing, with which it could fly around the top of a conical hill in one direction only. See FEARSOME CRITTERS.   (412)

Grylio In the medieval bestiary, an animal similar to the SALAMAN-DER, but which had a habit of climbing into apple trees and poisoning apples; these then poisoned the water if they happened to fall into a well.
(225)

Gudanna In Sumerian myth, when Gilgamish refused to marry Ishtar, she prevailed upon Anu to create Gudanna, the bull of heaven, in order to destroy him. But Gilgamish slew the animal with the help of his friend Enkidu, even though the monster destroyed two hundred men with each snort of his breath. (483)

Guirivulu South American cat-like monster armed with a claw-pointed tail. It lived in deep waters, attacking men and animals, becoming a serpent as it enveloped them. (489)

Guivre, *see* WIVRE

Gullinbursti ('gold bristle') A boar on which the god Freyr rode, or which drew his chariot. The creature was made by the dwarfs; he could run through the air and water better than any horse, and the glow from his mane and bristles was such that no matter how dark the night there was sufficient light wherever he went. The goddess Freyja also had a boar called Hildisvin (battle swine) and a third boar was called Slidringtanni (terrible tusk). The boar is especially associated with fertility deities.
(480)

Gulon Reported by Olaus Magnus in his description of Sweden (1555), the gulon was a cross between a hyena and a lioness, with very sharp claws and a long brown hairy body ending in a fox tail. This creature was

found in northern countries; in northern Sweden it was called a Jerff. The gulon had disgusting manners; he lived off dead carcasses which he devoured so violently that his belly swelled until 'it standeth out like a bell'. He then found two trees growing very close together and squeezed his body through, thereby pushing the meat through his body. This operation complete, he returned to begin again, and so the process went on until all was devoured. His flesh could not be eaten but his skin was prized for winter coats, and the only time that he could be captured was while he was wedged between two trees. His blood was also used, mingled with honey and drunk at weddings. The gulon came to symbolize the ultimate in gluttonous living. This traveller's tale had some basis in fact, since the glutton (*Gulo luscus*) is not unlike the beast described and is hunted for its skin only. (316)

Gumberoo   Larger than a bear, with a round leathery body that nothing could pierce; bullets ricocheted off its tough hide, and fire was the only thing that could kill a gumberoo. See FEARSOME CRITTERS. (412)

Guyascutus   Found in North America; this creature was reported in 1844 to be of gigantic proportions, inhabiting the tallest branches of the poplar tree. An early story tells how two showmen came to a small town in the Mid-West, and advertised the fearsome guyascutus or guyanoosa to be displayed that evening. The local people paid their money, and were waiting expectantly when one of the showmen rushed in crying 'De guyanoosa am loose!' Whereupon the audience departed hurriedly in one direction, while the showmen rode off with their money in the other direction. The creature shrank in size as time passed, and it eventually was described as being about the size of a white-tailed deer with ears like a rabbit and teeth like a mountain lion. Its unique feature was its telescopic legs which enabled it to graze on very steep pastures. It also had a safety device in its long tail which it wound round a rock when its legs failed to telescope. The early settlers in Vermont are reputed to have used the guyascutus to breed cattle with very short legs on one side for mountain pastures. The guyascutus were cherished by farmers as evidence of Providence's concern for their welfare. One man recalls a particularly affectionate guyascutus which frequently followed him to school, and how he cried miserably at the sight of the creature trying to walk on a road made for legs of equal length.

The guyascutus was also known as a sidewinder, hunkus, ricaboo racker, side-hill ganger, prock gwinter or cuter-cuss. The hunkus and the ricaboo racker were both able to turn themselves inside out when pursued and escape in the opposite direction. A creature of rather different dimensions was described in 1855 as a guyascutus; this was perfectly harmless and lived off hyacinth roots. It was three feet high, nine feet long with the tail adding an extra foot. Its back was covered with a shell composed of scales, or plates of a bony substance, forming a flexible but secure armour; it also had along the dorsal plates a row of short and powerful horns which extended from the shoulder to the loins.

A small clue to the idea from which the usual guyascutus developed comes from Sir Thomas Browne's *Pseudodoxia Epidemica*, where he says: 'That a Brock or Badger hath the legs on one side shorter than of the other, though an opinion perhaps not very ancient, is yet very general . . .' As prock gwinter is one of the alternative names, might not our old friend brock be at the bottom of the tale? (305, 412, 492)

Gwragedd Annwn Lake maidens found in Wales. They are very beautiful, but not so dangerous as mermaids. They frequently marry mortals and live happily. (413)

Gyes, *see* BRIAREUS

Hafgygr or **Margygr** A sea giantess, of the same type as the mother of Grendel in *Beowulf*, who haunted gloomy inland meres, and was described as 'a monster of a woman, she mourned her fate, she who had to live in the terrible lake, the cold water streams, after Cain slew his own brother.'

After her son's battle she had her revenge. Beowulf went in search of her in her watery home, where he saw 'many serpents in the water, strange sea dragons swimming in the lake and also water demons lying on cliff-ledges, monsters and serpents of the same kind as often in the morning molest ships on the sail-road'.

Beowulf dived into the lake, where he found Grendel's mother. After being attacked by the sea monsters, he engaged then in a fearsome combat at the bottom of the lake, and eventually Beowulf emerged victorious. (203)

Halcyon   A small bird with a long neck, bright blue in colour with a little white or purple in its plumage, taken by some to be a kingfisher. It was very rarely seen, usually at about the summer and winter solstices. It built its nest on the sea shore, and hatched its eggs in the midst of the winter storms. There was always a seven days' lull in the storms while the halcyon was brooding, and a further seven days while the chicks grew. These periods were known by sailors as halcyon days because the sea was calm and navigable, particularly the Sicilian sea. The halcyon had its origin in Greek mythology. Ceyx left his wife Alcyone to go on a voyage to consult the oracle of Apollo. Because Alcyone had annoyed Zeus, the god made a thunderstorm break over Ceyx's ship, and Ceyx was drowned. Alcyone learnt the news in a dream and in her distress went to the sea shore where she saw Ceyx's body. She was so distraught that she leapt into the sea and was drowned. At that point the pitying gods transformed her into a bird; as she sang a mournful song, Ceyx appeared and was changed into a bird too. For this reason the halcyon is symbolic of mourning.   (113, 118)

Halfway People   Known to the Micmac Indians of eastern Canada, these creatures had human upper parts, with a fish's form below. They sang before storms as a warning. If they were provoked they could conjure a storm, and inflict serious injury; however if well treated they were quite harmless.

Haokah   Giant thundergod of the Sioux Indians. Hot and cold were to him cold and hot; when he was miserable, he laughed, when he was happy, he cried. He had two different colours of skin on his face, and horns on his head.   (498)

Hanuman   An ancient monkey god of the Dravidian races adopted into Hindu mythology, he was the counterpart of Ganesha. He had a monkey's head on a human body, which was green, and a cow's tail. He was a demi-god and had particular qualities of speed, bravery and strength. He was reputed to have had his jaw broken by a thunderbolt sent by Indra, who was angry at his youthful attempts to reach the sun. It was also believed that he could stop the wind blowing. The monkey god tradition ran very deep; apes were sacred in India, and weddings of apes were celebrated at great expense as religious ceremonies. China too had a supernatural monkey which was indestructible and lived on jade juice, whose history is recounted in the story translated by Arthur Waley as *Monkey*. There were also other ape compound animals which were believed to exist in the sixteenth century; they included lion-apes, fox-apes, dog-apes and bear-apes, but were probably derived from over-graphic descriptions of various species of ape. (484)

Hare, Sea This creature had a hare's head and ears, but four fins behind the ears; it had a fish body, but hare's legs. In the sea it was a formidable creature, attacking anything within its range, but on land it became very timid. (405)

Harpies Foul birds with the head and breasts of women and the body and limbs of a vulture. Their claws were brazen, and they had metallic wings. The only thing they feared was a noise made with an instrument of their own brazen material. They lived in horrible places and had an insatiable hunger, which gave their faces a pale starved complexion. There was

no monster regarded as grimmer than a harpy, and no more wicked demon ever came up to the earth from the waters of the Styx. Everything they laid their hands on was contaminated by their disgusting stench. The most famous of the Greek legends with which they were connected involved Phineus, the blind King of Thrace who was doomed never to taste a meal from his own table because the harpies were sent to torment him and always snatched his meals before he had a chance to eat. They were driven away by two of the Argonauts and since Phineus' table was forbidden them they retreated to the Strophades islands. The harpies' name derives from the Greek for 'to seize'. (118, 428)

Hathor A primitive Egyptian sky goddess in the form of a cow whose legs are the points of the compass, wearing the sun-disc between her horns. In another, human form, as giver of eternal life, her tresses form the sky. Hathor came to be regarded as the Queen of Heaven and as such was patron of love and beauty. (490)

Haug-bui, *see* BARROW-WIGHT

Havfinë Norwegian mermaids whose tempers were quite unpredictable; they were sometimes kindly, but sometimes exceedingly cruel. When they were seen driving snow-white cattle up from the sea a storm was imminent. It was regarded as unlucky to see one of these mermaids. (517)

Hea-Bani Parallel to Chiron, the CENTAUR, in Sumerian legends, Hea-Bani appears as half-man, half-bull. The body, face and arms are human, the horns, legs, hoofs and tail are those of a bull. Hea-bani was celebrated for his wisdom. He met his end accidentally in a combat between Gizdhubar, his friend, and Humbaba. (108)

Hedley Kow A bogey known particularly to haunt the Northumbrian village of Hedley; he played numerous mischievous tricks by changing his form. He would become a truss of straw which got heavier and heavier when carried until the bearer was forced to put it down. He then shuffled away and a peal of laughter was heard. He could also turn himself into two things at once. He was known to become two pretty girls, who, encountering two young men, led them off into the bog and then vanished.

(413)

Hel The daughter of Loki in Scandinavian mythology, she was half flesh-coloured and half blue with a very stern forbidding aspect. Odin sent her down into the realms of mist and darkness known as Niflheim, where she had power over 'the nine regions' into which she distributed those who were sent to her, having died of disease or old age, instead of meeting an honourable end in battle.

(417)

Heliodromos, *see* PHOENIX

Hidebehind Always lurking behind trees, it particularly preyed on lumberjacks in North America. Because of its hiding nature it was never seen, but captured men and carried them off to its lair to eat them. See FEARSOME CRITTERS.

(412)

Hildirisin, *see* GULLINBURSTI

Hippocampus A sea-horse, half-horse, half-fish, ending in a dragon with a serpent's tail; he drew Poseidon's chariot. Now the generic term for the much smaller real-life seahorse. See also WATER-HORSE.

HIPPOCENTAUR

Hippocentaur, *see* CENTAUR

Hippocerf A compound creature, half-horse, half-stag. It symbolised indecision, since it was subjected to perpetual impulses pulling in contrary directions.

Hippogriff In Ariosto's *Orlando Furioso*, the hippogriff was the steed of the enchanter Atlantes, vanquished by Bradamante, later used by Rogero, her beloved. It was very beautiful but quite uncontrollable to ride.

> *But yet the beast he rode was not of art,*
> *But gotten of a* Griffeth *and a Mare*
> *And like a* Griffeth *had the former part*
> *As wings and head, and clawes that hideous are,*
> *And passing strength and force and ventrous hart,*
> *But all the rest may with a horse compare.*
> *Such beasts as these the hils of* Ryfee *yeeld*
> *Though in these parts they have bin seene but seeld.*

The wizard, fascinated by the foal, determined to tame it, and taught it to gallop to its goal whether on earth or in the heavens. No one else could control the creature. When Rogero was given the hippogriff the fairy Logistilla provided him with a magic bridle to control the beast. The scope for travel opened to Rogero was considerable. Instead of hastening to Bradamante, he resolved to visit other regions; he travelled the world, even to London (where he stopped to review a splendidly heraldic army); he then went to Ireland to rescue Angelica from the ORC. Later he destroyed the HARPIES in Ethiopia. Still with the hippogriff he ascended to the terrestrial paradise, then to Heaven, where he procured Orlando's lost wits (in a bottle) and restored the hero to his senses, or vice versa. Ariosto invented the beast from Virgil's metaphor 'to cross griffins with horses' (*Iungeant iam grypes equis*), meaning to attempt the impossible.

(303)

Hiyakudori Japanese two-headed bird, not unlike a bird of paradise; emblem of perfect love, it embodies the souls of two famous lovers. (460)

Hob or **Hobthrush**   A brownie, particularly found in Yorkshire and Durham. This brownie could cure children of whooping-cough. Parents took children to the Hobhole and said, 'Hobhole Hob, Hobhole Hob, my bairn's got kincough, tak't off! Tak't off!'   (413)

Hodag   Ferocious man-eating animal, with formidable horns, large bulging eyes, claws and a line of large sharp spikes which ran down the ridge of its back and long tail. It lived in dense swamps in Wisconsin. The hodag never lay down, but leant against a tree to sleep. It could only be captured by cutting deeply into the trunk of its favourite trees, and trapping it as it fell. See FEARSOME CRITTERS, and also compare ACHLIS.   (412)

Hoenir   Norse god, possibly originally the bird that laid the egg of the world. He is called 'long-legged', 'lord of the ooze', and the name is connected with Sanskrit for 'white bird', all ideas associated with the creator walking in chaos and finally hatching the egg of the world. Hoenir was a frequent companion of Odin and Loki, and was particularly noted for his silence.   (480)

Hog, Sea   This had a head like a hog, the teeth and tusks of a boar, a bending back like a 'creature begotten among swine'. Only the tail and hind part were like a fish, its four legs being those of a dragon. One was found in the North Sea in 1537. It was a very vicious creature, though the equivalent monster of the tropical seas had no legs and was not vicious. The latter was reputedly good to eat. Possibly some form of walrus is intended.   (321)

Hog Fish, *see* AMBIZE

Holy Fish, *see* EASG SAINT

Ho-o, *see* FENG-HWANG

Hoop Snake   This American snake puts its tail in its mouth and bowls along at high speed. The only way to escape it was to jump through the hoop, which so confused the creature that it rolled by and could not turn back. It may derive from the eternity-serpent symbol, known in Egyptian and Greek art. See FEARSOME CRITTERS.   (412)

Hornworm, *see* CERASTES

Horse, Neptune's It had brazen hoofs and a golden mane, and drew Neptune's chariot over the sea surrounded by a shoal of sea monsters. It is a simpler and later version of the HIPPOCAMPUS.   (417)

Horse, Oriental It was distinguished from ordinary horses by its verdant green mane and agate hooves and pasterns. Its coat was fringed with pearls, and its eyes were rubies. It is associated with Hindu traditions.
                                                                              (499)

Horse, Sea It had a head like a horse, and sometimes neighed; its feet were cloven like a cow's and its hind part was like a fish. It sometimes slept on ice floes; found mostly between Norway and Britain, it hunted for food both on land and in the sea.   (321)

Horses of the Sun In several mythologies, the sun was believed to travel across the sky in a chariot drawn by horses, which are variously named by ancient writers. In Graeco-Roman myth, Ovid refers to Pyrois, Eous, Aethon and Phlegon; an Armenian writer calls them Enik, Menik, Benik and Senik. Eumelus of Corinth calls them Eous, who turned the sky to make day and night, Aethiops, a flaming horse who parched the grain. These two horses were trace horses and were male. The females were yoke-bearing; they were Bronte, known as thunder, and Sterope who provided the lightning. In Scandinavian myth, there were two, Arrak and Alsvid; in Hindu myth only one is named, Etasa.   (113, 115, 485)

Horus Hawk-headed god of Egyptian mythology. He was the son of Osiris, who hunted Seth and eventually killed him; unfortunately he lost an eye in the process, which was later restored by Thoth. The eye of Horus features prominently in many Egyptian religious monuments. Horus was said to have eventually ascended the throne of Egypt.   (490)

Hounds of Annwn or Gabriel Hounds which hunted the souls of the damned to the northern Hell, a myth derived from the noisy summer migration of wild geese to the Arctic Circle.   (413)

Houyhnhnms Encountered by Gulliver on his travels, when he was being besieged by Yahoos, these creatures appeared to be horses, but were the presiding creatures of their nation, and the Yahoos (who in some degree resembled humans) were base servile animals. They were particularly renowned for their friendship and benevolence, and were never heard to express anything evil. They had a language of their own which Gulliver learnt in his sojourn with them. He posed a real problem to them, because, although resembling a Yahoo, he had none of the base habits of these animals. The Houyhnhnms used the hollow between the pastern and the hoof of the fore-leg as a hand, and could even thread a needle or milk a cow. They lived a very ordered life, keeping to the rules of the community, and, although they did not write, they were very exceptional poets.

Hraesvelg An eagle who caused winds to blow, in Norse mythology.

Hsiao A bird with an ape's body, a man's face and an animal tail. It was the opposite omen to the K'NEI, its appearance foretelling a lengthy drought. (411)

Hsing-t'ien This creature once fought against the Chinese gods, and was decapitated as a punishment. Its eyes were in its chest and its mouth in its navel; brandishing its weapons, it wandered endlessly in search of its head. (411)

Hua-hu Tiao In Chinese Buddhist myth, a creature carried by one of the Four Diamond Kings of Heaven in a panther-skin bag. When released, it became a white-winged elephant and devoured men. It was slain by Yang Chien, who rent it apart from within when it swallowed him. (518)

Huginn, *see* CREATURES OF ODIN

Huldra A Norse mountain fairy or wood nymph. She appeared as a beautiful woman, but had a long tail which she usually concealed. She lived in a mountain and watched her cattle. The Huldras were very musical folk; they played an enchanting unforgettable melody which caused great sadness. Some local peasants were said to have learnt the tune and to be able to play it. (427)

Humbaba The monstrous 'guardian of the mountain cedars' slain by Gilgamish in the Sumerian epic of Gilgamish. It wore seven cloaks, was horned like a wild bull, with lion's paws and vulture's claws. It was sometimes described as a kind of demon with a grotesque human face.

(108, 484)

Humma Like a bird of paradise, it was supposed by the Hindus to pass its whole life in the blue vault of heaven, never having any contact with earth. The humma was a good omen and was depicted over the throne of the Tippoo Sultan. (458)

Hunkus, *see* GUYASCUTUS

Huppe Similar to a peacock, to medieval writers this bird was in fact a cold-blooded fiend, capable of perpetrating the most horrible acts. It attached great importance to possessions, and guarded them jealously. It had no clan feeling but lived an independent life. Its only commendable quality was its concern for its parents in old age. (458)

Hydra A monster born of ECHIDNE and TYPHON and reared by Hera. This marsh-dwelling creature had a prodigious dog-like body with

heads ranging from seven to nine in number, although some authorities will credit it with anything up to a thousand heads. Of these snaky heads one is immortal: if any are cut off, new ones multiply in their place. The very breath of this monster or smell of its track could destroy life, as it is an impersonation of the plague. The second labour of Hercules was to slay the Lernean Hydra which he did by burning off its heads, thus preventing the blood from sprouting new heads, and burying the last immortal head under a rock. The hydra appears in heraldic devices as a many-headed dragon.

Hydrippus According to medieval bestiaries, this creature had the front part of a horse, but from the haunches the form of a fish. He was the leader of all fish. In the east there lived a gold-coloured fish with burnished scales, which never left home. The hydrippus led all fish to it, who greeted it as a king. Those fish who did not follow it inevitably landed up in fishermen's nets.   (204)

Hyman Topodes According to Solinus this goat-like creature was found in Libya. It had curious legs which were so jointed as to make them completely bowed. The result was that the creature could not pick up its feet like other animals but was forced to shuffle or creep along the ground in a painstaking fashion. His Elizabethan translator, Arthur Golding, called it a Goatfete Crookelegs.   (119)

Ichthyocentaurs Followers of Pan, these were winged creatures, half-fish, half-horse.

Ihuaivulu In the myths of the South American Indians, this seven-headed fire monster inhabits volcanic neighbourhoods, and presumably contributes to the eruptions.   (489)

Ipopodes A lesser kind of centaur, found in Scythia; instead of having horses' bodies and human trunks, only their legs and feet were equine. (315)

Iriz Ima, *see* MOKÊLE-MBÊMBE

Jabberwock   '*The Jabberwock with eyes of flame*
Came miffling through the tulgey wood
And burbled as it came'

only to find that its creator, Lewis Carroll, had reserved no better fate for it than the point of a 'vorpal blade'.

Jalpan   Seductive, dangerous water-nymph of the Punjab.   (470)

Jeduah, *see* VEGETABLE LAMB OF TARTARY

Jenny Greenteeth   A malignant water creature found in Lancashire, which attacks and drowns the unwary; the only sign of its presence is a green scum on the water.   (413)

Jenny Haniver   Any manufactured monster rejoices in this name, which may come from Antwerp (Anvers), the home of many such creations. A favourite basis was a skate or ray, whose outspread form could be made to resemble wings; many leathery DRAGONS began life as one or other of these fish, and BASILISKS were formed from similar materials. Alternatively, two parts of ordinary species could be sewn together to make a MERMAID or other creature. More recent examples came from the United States and date from 1929 to 1933; they were produced by fishermen who had never heard of either Jenny Hanivers or basilisks.   (301, 473)

Jinns   In Muslim mythology, these creatures are said to have inhabited earth before man, having been created from fire. They rebelled against God under their leader Azael, and were banished to the deserts. Being

90

chiefly spiritual beings they can change forms rapidly and rarely appear to men, though animals can see them. They move only by night, mounted on animals, but are usually themselves represented as half-wolf, half-hyena. (483)

JinshinUwo The earthquake-fish on the back of which Japan is popularly supposed to float, the lashing of whose tail causes tremors. A large stone in the garden of the temple of Kashima is said to rest on its back, and is the rivet that holds the world together. Cf. VARAHA. (463)

Jormungandr In Scandinavian legend, a serpent who encircled the earth, Cf. MIDGARD-SERPENT. (436)

Jubjub A creature encountered during the hunting of the SNARK; it terrified the stalwart snark seekers. Chiefly distinguished by its voice, it was described as a

'desperate bird
Since it lives in perpetual passion:
Its taste in costume is entirely absurd—
It is ages ahead of the fashion:

'But it knows any friend it has met once before:
It never will look at a bribe:
And in charity-meetings it stands at the door,
And collects – though it does not subscribe.'

Jumar According to John Baptist Porta's sixteenth-century treatise, *Natural Magick*, this is the offspring of a bull and an ass: scientifically an improbable if not impossible creature, and hence fabulous. (319)

Kakamora Dwarf-like forest creatures with long sharp nails and straight hair found in the forests of the Pacific Islands. They are variously described as between six inches and five feet high. They were known to kill and eat men, but feared anything white; and it is said that they have now all been captured. (470)

Kama Itachi Japanese invisible weasel who carried a sickle and would inflict cuts or scratches for no reason. Any such injury whose cause was unknown or could not be talked about was blamed on this creature, as were broken sandal-straps. (463)

Kappa Japanese river goblin with the body of a tortoise and scaly limbs. On the top of its ape-like head was a cavity filled with the fluid which gave it strength. It preyed on humans, and could only be over-come by politeness: if, on meeting a kappa, one bowed, the kappa would return the compliment and spill the fluid from the top of its head. (499)

Kar-fish In Zoroastrian myth these guard the tree of immortality (Gaokerena) created by Ahura-Mazda, which is constantly attacked by the lizard of the evil spirit (Angra Mainyu). The struggle will last until the universe itself is renewed. The kar-fish circle round the tree, so that the head of one of their number is always turned towards the lizard: their eyesight is so keen that they can detect a ripple no thicker than a hair. (484)

Kargas, *see* GRIFFIN

Kaukas, *see* PUK

Kelpie, *see* WATER-HORSE

Khubilgan Any animal or bird which acted as the spirit-protector of a Siberian shaman or medicine-man. Often the killing of a khubilgan, or soul-animal, resulted in the shaman's own death, and if the khubilgans of two shamans fought, the one associated with the losing animal would fall gravely ill. The relationship between shaman and khubilgan is similar to that of a witch and her familiar. (482)

Khumbaba, *see* HUMBABA

Kiau A sea-serpent which infested the Chien-Tang river in China; killed by a local hero in A.D. 1129.

K'i-lin, *see* CH'I-LIN

Kirni, *see* GRIFFIN

Kirtimukha In Hindu myth, the Face of Glory. It is depicted as a lion's face without a body and limbs; there is no chin, the eyes protrude, and the thick eyebrows extend to resemble horns. A halo of flame-like bushy hair is balanced by a yawning, cavernous mouth. In the version found in Javanese doorways, pearls and flowers spring from the mouth, which end in MAKARA heads.

A similar monster-mask, the T'ao-tieh, supposed to drive away evil spirits, was much used on early Chinese sacrificial bronzes. The apparition itself was said to have been banished to outer darkness by the Emperor Shin in the second millennium B.C.

The Hindus relate that the Face of Glory was the result of the anger of the god Siva, when he received a message saying that he was unworthy to marry his beloved, Parvati. In his rage, a man-lion monster sprang from his forehead, which turned on Siva and demanded prey. Siva suggested that he ate himself: which he obligingly did, leaving only his face and a string of pearls which had been his entrails. The god then appointed him guardian of doorways, and commanded that he should be worshipped and offered sacrifices of meat.   (477)

K'nei A one-legged sheep found in a well and brought to Confucius as being an omen. Confucius correctly predicted that heavy rains would follow. See HSIAO.   (519)

Koori and **Bucu** The two mystic birds which enable the Siberian shaman or medicine-man to travel to the spirit world; Koori bears his soul, Bucu acts as a protective escort.   (482)

Kraken This gigantic creature was reputedly found off the Norwegian coast, where in the sixteenth century fishermen reported that on hot days they used to take soundings when a few miles offshore and find that the depth of water was only five fathoms instead of fifteen or twenty. At the same time, they began to catch an abundance of fish. If the bottom got shallower, this meant that the kraken which was lying there was about to

KRAKEN

awake: they would row to a safe distance, and the monster eventually emerged. It was about a mile and a half in length, with points or horns which emerged like masts; these were its arms. It was very strong and would easily wreck a man of war. As it descended again there was a great whirlpool.

More learned writers stated that its body could never be found, because there were only two of the species, which would live until Doomsday. The bishop of Nidros had once celebrated Mass on its back, and it had remained immobile throughout the ceremony.

On the other hand, there have been various reports of stranded krakens, and a young kraken was trapped in the reefs of Alstadhang in 1680, though no details survive; and it was seen at Rothesay on the Isle of Bute in 1775, having presumably wandered from its usual habitat. Most washed-up krakens were probably giant squid, which were to suffer epidemics of stranding off Newfoundland and New Zealand in the late nineteenth century. Even the monstrous kraken has much in common with the giant squid. And there is an echo of the false bottom that it caused at sea in the modern theory that myriads of small squid cause the phenomenon of the 'deep scattering layer' – a false bottom picked up by echo-sounders. In one of his early poems, Tennyson paints a vivid picture of the Kraken:

> Below the thunders of the upper deep,
> Far, far beneath in the abysmal sea,
> His ancient, dreamless, uninvaded sleep
> The Kraken sleepeth: faintest sunlights flee
> About his shadowy sides; above him swell
> Huge sponges of millennial growth and height;
> And far away into the sickly light,
> From many a wondrous grot and secret cell
> Unnumber'd and enormous polypi
> Winnow with giant arms the slumbering green.
> There hath he lain for ages and will lie
> Battening upon huge seaworms in his sleep,
> Until the latter fire shall heat the deep;
> Then once by men and angels to be seen,
> In roaring he shall rise and on the surface die.

(318, 429, 454, 495)

94

LAMIAE

Kreutzet   Bird found in Muscovy similar to an eagle but much larger; it terrorised all other birds. In Poland it was called Bialozar. Cf. ROC, SIMURGH. (301)

Kudan   A Japanese creature which always told the truth, depicted as a bull with a man's head, three eyes on each flank and horns along its back.

Kukulkan Another name for QUETZALCOAT.

Kulili   One of the dragons of Chaos in the myths of Sumeria, conquered by the god Marduk. He reappears as a fish-man on late Assyrian seals, and is a forerunner of the Greek figure of the zodiac, Aquarius the water-bearer. (483)

Kundrav, *see* GANDAREVA

Kylin, *see* CH'I-LIN

Lamassus, *see* SEDUS

Lamiae   Lamia was one of the mistresses of Zeus; her children were killed by the jealous Hera, and as a result the distraught mother took to destroying other women's children. She was also associated with the blood-sucking vampires called EMPUSAE. Her descendants were creatures with the heads and breasts of women, but their bodies were those of a four-footed animal, with claws in front and cloven hooves at the back. They sucked human blood, particularly from children. Another account gave them serpents' bodies, and said that they were the swiftest of all human animals. In the Middle Ages they were confused with the gorilla or some similar creature: these lamiae lived in forests and deserted places, emerging at night. They made a great disturbance, breaking off branches and biting any human who approached, the wounds only being cured if the victim heard the lamia's roar. In appearance they were goat-like, with horses' hooves. They could take the form of mermaids and sink ships, according to another version. Finally they were mistaken for the empusae as well, and given shape-changing powers: usually they took the shape of beautiful harlots, but they hissed like dragons, which betrayed their real nature. (115, 201)

Lavellan A beast found in Scotland which had a head like a rat or mouse, and a body of the same colour. It was able to injure cattle merely by its presence from a distance of thirty yards or more, but they could be cured by dipping its skin in their water. The water-vole was supposed to have similar powers. (509)

Lemers A creature the size of a mouse found in Norway, which dropped from thunderclouds and locustlike devoured all green things. It was probably a lemming, whose self-destructive urge is linked with the fact that the multiplying numbers of the species cause food shortages at intervals. (306)

Leontophonus According to Aldrovandus, no one has left an adequate description of these small creatures, 'the bane of lions', so called because their flesh was fatal to lions. Even the ashes of the leontophonus placed at a crossroads would kill lions if they ate a very small amount, and hunters used its ashes on pieces of meat to poison lions. The lion, if it met one, would blind it and kill it with a blow to avoid biting it. (118, 401)

Leprechaun The most famous tribe of Irish fairies, they appeared as dwarfs less than two feet tall. They haunted wine-cellars and were reputedly guardians of immense treasure.

Leucrocotta Pliny calls it 'a wild beast of extraordinary swiftness, the size of a wild ass, with the legs of a stag, the neck, tail and breast of a lion, the head of a badger, a cloven hoof, the mouth slit up as far as the ears, and one continuous bone instead of teeth'. According to Solinus its cry 'counterfeiteth the speech of man', and it seems to be a species of hyena. (118)

Leviathan The great fish of the deeps in Hebrew myth, symbol of God's power: in *The Book of Job*, chapter 41, he is described: 'His scales are his pride, shut up together as with a close seal . . . Out of his mouth go burning lamps, and sparks of fire leap out . . . He esteemeth iron as straw, and brass as rotten wood . . . He maketh the deep to boil like a pot: he maketh the sea like a pot of ointment. He maketh a path to shine after him; one would think the deep to be hoary [covered in hoar-frost]. Upon earth there is not his like, who is made without fear.' Like the MIDGARD-SERPENT, he encircled the earth; but he also had as many eyes as the year has days; he fed off dragons three hundred leagues in length. The Islamic equivalent is called Nun. The most powerful of all cabalistic spells is that which summons Leviathan, who was fashioned together with Behemoth on the fifth day of the creation. God played with him during the last quarter of each day, and the river Jordan emptied itself into his mouth. At the Day of Judgement his flesh will be food for the righteous and part of his skin will make a tent for them. The rest will cover the walls of Jerusalem, where its brightness will be visible to the ends of the earth. See also TARASQUE.   (410, 444)

Lindorm A snake-like creature, which devoured cattle and ate bodies. Known to invade churches and churchyards, it could only be removed with great difficulty because of its huge size. The lindworm is a heraldic dragon or wyvern without wings, presumably the same as the lindorm.
(427)

Lions Heraldic lions are sometimes found with two or three bodies, or two heads in a kind of shorthand notation, or even compounded with a wyvern. The winged lion of St Mark is one of the Four Evangelic Creatures, the others being the ox of St Matthew, the eagle of St John and the man of St Luke.   (314)

Liver A bird said to have frequented the pool near which Liverpool was built. It is depicted in the arms of Liverpool as a cormorant-like creature.
(515)

Lokapala elephants In Tantric myth, the world is supported by eight beings called Lokapalas, who ride on horned elephants with birds' bodies.   (507)

97

Loyres Sir John Mandeville says that the inhabitants of the kingdom of Maney use these animals to catch fish for them from rivers as a means of obtaining food: it could be a confused reminiscence of the oriental use of cormorants by fishermen. (219)

Lucidius or **Lumerpa** A bird from Asia which, according to one Book of Beasts, shone so brightly that it absorbed its own shadow. Even after death it continued to give out light, but if feathers were plucked from it, these ceased to shine. See also ERCINE; owls have also been observed to become luminous after roosting in rotten trees, the spores of some fungi being phosphorescent. (214, 228)

Lufferlang An American FEARSOME CRITTER with triple-jointed legs and a bushy tail growing out of the middle of its back. It could run equally fast in any direction. (412)

Lung Wang The Chinese dragon king: bringer of rain, ruler of the oceans, he dwelt in all lakes, and controlled the storms. He was particularly associated with waterspouts. (470)

Lurikeen, *see* NISSE

Lybbarde A partly fictitious creature, being a confused description of a leopard. Supposedly the offspring of a lioness and a panther, it became the heraldic symbol of boldness. (515)

Lycaon A wolf with a mane on his neck, 'so pied', says Solinus, 'that men say there is no colour but he hath part of it'. (119)

Lympago Heraldic creature, half-man, half-lion or tiger.

Lyons-Bane, *see* LEONTOPHONUS

Lyon-Poisson Half-lion, half-fish, a compound monster sometimes found in heraldry. (476)

Makara   The word means sea-monster, and the creature has been variously identified as a shark, dolphin, crocodile or crab; in Indian folk-lore it appeared as a giant crab. Hindu myth equated it with the zodiac sign Capricorn, and it was on a makara that Varuna and Ganga rode. As steed of Varuna, lord of water, it was half-bird, half-crocodile; it also carried Vishnu in the guise of half-antelope, half-fish. The term was also used of composite monsters in general: hence elephant, fish, dragon, goat and other makaras are found, but there is always a mammal and a fish present in the composite parts, and it has a snout of some sort. It may derive from the Babylonian god EA, and its dual nature represents the balance of good and evil in nature.   (470, 477)

Manabozho or **Manabush**   The Great Hare in the legends of the Algonquin Indians of North America, who was the incarnation of life-giving energy. He was the creator and provider of food, and chief of medicine-men. Among his exploits were the destruction of the great fish, representing evil, with the aid of the THUNDERBIRDS; he was swallowed by it and cut his way out. He also stole fire from the sun-god and gave it to men. He now lives on the world's edge in the far west in the village of souls.   (488)

Manasa   Literally mind or thought. A Hindu snake-goddess, especially worshipped in Bengal, who is yellow in colour, four-armed and clothed in snakes, and sits on a waterlily. She is known as 'she who does no cooking', and no fires are kindled at her festival; her devotees play with snakes at this celebration, which often results in fatal bites.   (470)

Mandrake   This was a root similar to a miniature man in appearance, and only took on animal, or rather human, form in black magic ceremonies, as described in Lawrence Durrell's *Balthazar*.

Man-Lion, Man-Tiger, *see* KIRTIMUKHA, LYMPAGO

99

Mantichora, Manticory, Marticoras (also **Memecoleous, Maricomorion, Mantiserra**) From the Persian *mardkhora*, man-slayer; it is probably a man-eating tiger, as Pausanias recognised. Aristotle quoted Ctesias, Alexander's physician, whose own works are now lost: 'He assures us that the Indian wild beast called the "marticoras" has a triple row of teeth in both upper and lower jaw; that it is as big as a lion and equally hairy, and that its feet resemble those of the lion; that it resembles man in its face and ears; that its eyes are blue, and its colour

vermilion; that its tail is like that of the land-scorpion; that it has a sting in the tail, and has the faculty of shooting off arrow-wise the spines that are attached to the tail; that the sound of its voice is something between the sound of a pan-pipe and that of a trumpet; that it can run swiftly as a deer, and that it is as savage as a man-eater.' In modern Spanish folklore, the manticore is a kind of werewolf who eats children. This terrifying creature was a particular favourite with sixteenth- and seventeenth-century illustrators. (101, 104, 116, 228, 322)

Mara Old English for demon: hence nightmare, mare's nest. It could be a giant, dwarf, or elfin woman depending on the type of dream; it entered the room through any small cranny, and died if the cranny was blocked and it could not escape at dawn. Women were believed to become demons of this sort and under ecclesiastical law a woman acting as a nightmare and 'riding' a man or his servants was fined or outlawed. (413)

MERMAIDS

Margygr, *see* HAFGYGR, MERMAIDS

Matsya A horned fish, the first incarnation of Vishnu in Hindu myth.
(469)

Maugmolach or **Hairy Meg** This spirit like a BANSHEE appeared only at Tullochgrim, where it gave warning of the approaching death of members of the Clan Grant. (413)

Medusa The chief of the GORGONS, whose head was later used by Perseus to slay his enemies by turning them to stone. (115)

Melusine A water-sprite, who is occasionally depicted in British heraldry as a mermaid with two tails; the central character in the French medieval tale of the fair Melusine. See MERMAIDS, below. (439)

Mermaids These bewitching creatures are usually shown as beautiful long-haired women with a fish's tail from the waist down, holding a comb and mirror. Like the SIRENS, their song was enchanting and alluring: it has become a poetic symbol for the power of music. Oberon speaks of it in *A Midsummer Night's Dream* (II i):

> 'once I sat upon a promontory
> And heard a mermaid on a dolphin's back
> Uttering such dulcet and harmonious breath
> That the rude sea grew civil at her song
> And certain stars shot madly from their spheres
> To hear the sea-maid's music.'

The sea-maid in European tradition goes back to the fish-gods of ancient Babylon, such as EA and ATARGATIS. Atargatis was a Semitic moon-goddess who seems to be the first recorded mermaid; but her child, Semiramis, was a normal human, and this made her mother so ashamed that she killed her lover and abandoned the infant, for which she became wholly a fish. The tradition has been strongly reinforced by seafaring lore, to which the mermaid really belongs. The seal is at the root of the many Norwegian and Hebridean legends about mermaids; and she has been

MERMAIDS

confused again with the seal-maid proper, who comes ashore and casts her skin. If her skin is removed, she is compelled to remain in human shape, like the swan-maid. Mermaids who took human lovers more frequently exacted a vow of secrecy from them, which if broken meant their return to the water, a condition on which the medieval French romance of Melusine turns. In the Orkneys, however, the sea-trows, a fey race of surpassing beauty, behaved like the seal-maid, and could be captured by taking their cast skin from them.

The comb and mirror seem to belong to the SIRENS rather than mermaids proper: the comb, so Robert Graves has suggested, may have been a plectrum (for plucking a stringed instrument), and the mirror could be the instrument itself in a distorted form. Against this, the Babylonian mer-creatures were highly cultivated: one of them is supposed to have taught the Babylonians arts and sciences, and the mermaid's musical talent could derive from this.

Mermaids have no souls, and longed to acquire them; if they were able to transform themselves into spirits of the air, they could win souls at the end of three hundred years if they behaved themselves. On Iona, round smooth pebbles were said to be the tears of a mermaid who had begged one of the saints on the island to give her a soul, but had been refused. This reluctance on the holy man's part was probably due to the mermaid's reputation for luring men to their deaths: for (again like the sirens) she was a *femme fatale*. 'I'll drown more sailors than the mermaid can' says Richard III in *Henry VI*, Part II. Local traditions often attached their appearances to particularly dangerous spots, reefs or rocks, and the mermaid is usually shown, not like Shakespeare's, on a dolphin, but seated on a rock. They could also raise storms at will, a tradition also attached to the HALFWAY PEOPLE of the Micmac Indians in Canada who are half-men, half-fish, but who only inflict such injuries if angered.

Being one of the most widely known of fabulous creatures, and yet not a rarity like the phoenix or unicorn, reports of sightings and captures were frequent. Although medieval chroniclers occasionally record their appearance – one was supposedly captured at Orford in the twelfth century – their heyday was in the eighteenth and nineteenth centuries. Captured specimens which were displayed were JENNY HANIVERS of some kind or another.

Mermen and merwomen, as opposed to mermaids, were less attractive.

The MARGYGR was horrible to look upon, with squat features and piercing eyes. As it was reported from Greenland, it may well have been a walrus, though an Icelandic version relates it to the kraken. Another merman was a kind of club bore; he had fin-like legs, and was very loquacious in that he would rise from the water and address anyone who happened to be near.

Mermaids are only one of a variety of water-sprites such as the tangie in the Orkneys: see also APSARAS, DRAC, NIX, PEG POWLER, MORUADH, NYMPHS, SIRENS, WATER-HORSE. The Japanese Ningyo is depicted as a fish with a human head. (517)

Merrows An Irish people who lived on dry land below the sea, and passed through the water by means of their enchanted caps. The women were very beautiful, but the males were red-nosed and pig-eyed, with green hair and teeth and a penchant for brandy. It was perhaps the last trait that made the females so eager to marry humans. (464)

Merrymaids   Cornish for MERMAIDS.

Meshekenabec   A great lake serpent, identical with the great fish killed by MANABOZHO. He dwelt with his many monstrous attendants in the lake of Manitous; his body was covered with hard glistening scales of every colour, his head was red and his eyes glowed.   (454)

Metacollinarum   An unspecified creature found in the 'Three Indies' according to the fabulous epistle from Prester John, a twelfth-century forgery supposed to be a letter from the great ruler of the East.   (429)

Mice, Giant   William Caxton's translation of the encyclopaedia *Speculum Mundi* (Mirror of the World) says that in India 'there ben yet myes the whiche ben as grete as cattes and also swyft in rennyng', a report which might have been more credible if he had been referring to the capybaras or coypus of the New World.   (206)

Microbe   *The Microbe is so very small*
You cannot make him out at all,
But many sanguine people hope
To see him through a microscope.
His jointed tongue which lies beneath
A hundred curious rows of teeth;
His seven tufted tails have lots
Of lovely pink and purple spots,
On each of which a pattern stands,
Composed of forty separate bands;
His eyebrows of a tender green;
All these have never yet been seen—
But Scientists, who ought to know,
Assure us that it must be so . . .
Oh! let us never, never doubt
What nobody is sure about!

Hilaire Belloc, *Cautionary Tales*

Midgard-Serpent In Scandinavian myth, the child of Loki, the evil god, Jormungandr, a serpent monster so vast that when Odin threw him into the deep ocean he encircled the earth. At the end of the world when the day of Ragnarök comes, he will rise against the gods, to be killed by Thor, who will himself be suffocated by the midgard-serpent in the struggle.   (438)

Miehts-hozjin The 'master of the forest' in Lapland, who loved silence above all. If anyone shouted, sang or made a noise in the forest, the miehts-hozjin, a black creature with a tail, would bewilder him so that he lost his way.   (482)

Milamo A super-crane so large that it could swallow earth-worms as large as the inner tubes of car tyres. See FEARSOME CRITTERS.
                                                                                                  (412)

Mimick Dog A creature which could imitate anything, said to be descended from an ape, with a hedgehog-like face. They were common in Egypt in Ptolemy's time, and were used instead of servants in poor men's

houses. They were probably a species of monkey, especially as players are said to have used them in public spectacles.   (322)

Minotaur The King of Crete, Minos, begged Poseidon to send him a sign of his sovereignty, at which a bull appeared from the sea. Minos failed to sacrifice it, in revenge for which Poseidon made his wife Pasiphae fall in love with it, and the union was consummated with the aid of Daedalus, who also built the labyrinth in which the monstrous creature born of this union was kept. It was a bull-headed man, fed on the tribute of seven maidens and seven youths exacted from the Athenians. It was slain by Theseus, who won the love of Minos' daughter Ariadne. She told him how to kill it and gave him a skein of thread with which to retrace his way through the maze.   (479)

Minocane or **Homocane** A creature found in English heraldry, half-child, half-spaniel.

Mirmecoleon, *see* ANT-LION

Mirror Creatures Jorge Luis Borges in his *Book of Imaginary Beings* elaborates a Chinese superstition to describe how, in the days of the Yellow Emperor in China, the world of mirrors and the world of men were not separated and identical as they are now. The mirror world possessed as many different creatures, colours and shapes as the human world. The two worlds lived in peace, and mirrors were used as the gateways between them, until one night the creatures of the mirror world invaded the human world. All the magic of the Yellow Emperor was needed to repel them, and the defeated world was reduced to a servile reflection. One day they will perhaps shake off the spell and conquer the human world at their second attempt. The parallel with modern theories about anti-matter seems to be due to Borges's embroidery on the original theme of the fish which appeared in mirrors, presumably because the latter looked like pools of liquid.   (411)

Mixcoatl The Cloud-Serpent in Aztec myth. He was originally a dragon rain god but later became a huntsman. He was also god of lightning.   (508)

Mock Turtle The mock turtle is compounded of veal disguised as turtle, just as mock turtle soup is made of veal; so he has a turtle's shell but the head, hooves and tail of a calf. He appears with the GRYPHON in *Alice in Wonderland*.

Mokêle-Mbêmbe   A beast the size of an elephant with similar skin and colouring, found in West Africa and the Congo. It has a long flexible neck, one huge tooth or horn, and a muscular reptile's tail. Although it attacks canoes, it lives in caves, and goes ashore to search for its vegetarian food. Other beasts of the same ilk are the Groot Slang, and the Iriz Ima.

(473)

Monicodiata   A bird found in the Moluccas 'which having no feet is in continual motion. . . . There is a hole in the back of the Cock, in which the Hen doth lay her eggs, and hatch her young ones. I bid no man to believe these relations.' Thus Peter Heylin in the seventeenth century.

(311)

Monk-Calf   A deformed calf born at Freiberg in December 1522, apparently with monk's cowl and tonsure, and entirely black. Regarded as a dire omen, it was variously interpreted as a symbol of Luther himself (an ex-monk), the depravity of monks in general and a harbinger of war and disaster, the last according to Luther. See PAPSTESEL.   (315, 465)

Monk Fish   A type of merman sometimes found stranded on northern shores and widely exhibited, the monk fish had a closely shaven head, with a variation of a monk's hood on its shoulders, two pinnate fins for arms, while the lower part of its body ended in a long curving fish-tail. Reported from the thirteenth century onwards, good specimens were seen in 1531, and at Copenhagen in 1549. These latter were probably JENNY HANIVERS. See also BISHOP FISH.   (464)

Monoceros   (1) A single-horned beast somewhere between a rhinoceros and the unicorn. Pliny gives it a stag's head, elephant's feet and a boar's tail, and says that the rest is like a horse. It makes a deep lowing noise and has a single short black horn in its forehead, about a foot long. 'This animal, it is said, cannot be taken alive', he adds. A medieval description agrees in most details, but says that it howls horribly instead of lowing.   (118, 228)

(2) A single-horned fish that can pierce through a ship. It is very slow, which makes it less alarming than it might otherwise be. Probably a narwhal, whose horns were the chief source of unicorn relics.   (321)

Monoscelans, *see* SCIAPODS

Moon-Rabbit The Aztecs believed that the moon was once as bright as the sun until the latter darkened the rival source of light by casting a rabbit on his face. The Buddhists tell of the hare who sacrificed himself to appease Buddha's hunger; in reward his soul was sent to the moon, where he sits making the elixir of life. (484, 519)

Morholt In the romance of Tristan and Isolde, Tristan fights the Morholt, a knight of superhuman powers and champion of Ireland, in order to free Cornwall from the tribute paid to the Irish king. Originally the Morholt was probably a monster from which he rescued Isolde, perhaps dragon-like. (502)

Moruadh or **Moruach** *see* MERROWS

Muircartach Irish 'hag of the sea': she was bald, coal-coloured face with one goggle eye in forehead. Possibly an impersonation of the storm. (509)

Muninn, *see* CREATURES OF ODIN

Murrisk A sea-fish which inhabited the plain near Croagh Patrick. This amphibious being was exceedingly unpleasant: if it spewed in the water all the fishes died, if it belched fumes it killed all the birds, and if it breathed vapour over the land it killed all living things like a plague. (430)

Muryans Cornish fairies, originally larger than humans, which (in expiation of some unspecified crime) were condemned to diminish each year until they became ants and then died. (413)

Mushrush, *see* SIRRUSH

Mushussu One of the eleven dragons under TIAMAT in Sumerian myth; serpent-like, triple-jawed and three-headed, it was identified with the consellation Hydra. (483)

Musimon or **Musimus** Cross between ram and she-goat; goat-like, but with horns of both species. (515)

Nāgā Semi-divine beings with human heads and serpent bodies, in some respects identified with the Nāgā tribe of north-east India, who were reputed to have shape-changing powers. They were not necessarily evil, and could only harm humans who molested them, though their aspect could be terrible, many-headed, multi-coloured and ferocious. They dwelt either in the depths of the earth, in Nāgāloka, or according to other reports in the underwater city of Bhagavati, where their palaces were jewel-studded, filled with flowers, and there was always dancing and singing. The daughters sometimes married humans; and descent from these beautiful nagini was often claimed by minor Indian princely families. Garuda was their mortal enemy, and when they left their abode they were in dire danger of being attacked by him. The Nepalese believed them to control the weather; a local saint was once foolish enough to shut nine nāgās up in a hillock, and a drought followed, lasting twelve years. (470, 436, 484)

Naiads, *see* NYMPHS

Näkk (Estonian), **Näkki** (Finnish), **Näcken** (German), *see* NIX

Nandi The milk-white bull on which the Hindu god Siva rides.

Narasinha The fourth avatar of the Hindu god Vishnu. A certain Hiranyakasipu had been granted immunity from being killed by any man or animal because of his devout life. However, he hated Vishnu, and when his son affirmed that Vishnu was present everywhere, he struck a pillar of the palace asking whether Vishnu was in it. At this, Vishnu emerged from the pillar as Narasinha a man-lion and tore the unbeliever asunder. (484)

Nependis A heraldic creature, half-ape, half-swine. (476)

Nereids, *see* NYMPHS

Nesnas A one-eyed, one-legged, one-handed creature, like a human being divided in half, found in Southern Arabia. Its habits were similar to those of the EMPUSAE. See also DIREACH GHLINN EITIDH.

Nidhogg The dragon that lay at the roots of Yggdrasil, the Scandinavian ash-tree that supports the world. The squirrel Ratatosk bore 'envious words' between him and the eagle that sat on top of Yggdrasil, and 'knew many things'. (480)

Nisse Beings the size of small children, dressed in grey. They lived in barns and stables and cared for horses and cattle. They were not always easy and might favour one animal or let out others. Sweetmeats were left for them on Christmas Eve. Like the Irish Lurikeen they would sometimes indicate where buried treasure might be found.

Nix or **Nixie** The nix was a water-sprite, treacherous to men. The female was siren-like, beautiful, sometimes fish-tailed, and lured men to drown: the male was usually old and dwarfish but sometimes appeared as a golden-haired boy or, in Iceland and Sweden, as a centaur. His slit ears and cloven feet distinguished him, and he always hid his feet. He loved music and would play enchantingly on the harp. If he appeared as a horse (see WATER-HORSE), he would tempt someone to mount him and drown them by dashing into the water. He demanded annual human sacrifices, but sometimes, like the mermaid, intensely desired to obtain a soul.

Another variety of nixies was more elfin; they occasionally appeared as wives in the market, betrayed by the wet edge of their aprons. If they paid well, everything would be expensive that year; if badly, goods would be cheap. Both sometimes married humans, but the result was always tragic. See also PEG POWLER. (477)

Nuckelavee Centaur-like Irish sea monster with breath that brought plague, and with no skin. The only way to escape from it was to cross running water, which it could not abide. (413)

Nun, *see* LEVIATHAN

Nunyenunc A vast bird which carried off men among the mountain Indians of North America: distinct from THUNDERBIRDS. (488)

Nykur, *see* WATER-HORSE

Nymphs   General name for spirits of a particular place: Nereids or Oceanides were the nymphs of the sea and ocean; mountain nymphs were Oreads, tree nymphs Dryads (dwelling among trees) or Hamadryads (spirits of one particular tree), nymphs of springs and pools Naiads. As a race they were all beautiful and capricious: they could cast spells and occasionally steal children. They could be cruel at times, and some, like satyrs, were goat-footed. The whirlwind was said to be a nymph passing by. Nereids, Naiads and Oreads were immortal; Dryads and Hamadryads died when trees were felled.

Oannes, *see* EA

Oats Goat   A harvest spirit whose function was similar to that of the corn dolly in England. In order to ensure a fruitful season, it was honoured at the Shrovetide feast in Bohemia, when a mummer represented it. In Bavaria the same spirit appeared as a stallion, elsewhere in Germany as a bear (see SHROVETIDE BEAR).   (470)

Oceanides, *see* NYMPHS

Odontotyrannus   A vast beast with three horns on its forehead, which lived in the Ganges. It was amphibious and so large that it could swallow an elephant whole: it hated men, and even fire and arrows would not deter it from attacking them. Alexander the Great, in a romantic account of his Eastern conquests, was said to have lost twenty-six men to one of these black monsters.   (408)

O Goncho   A white dragon which lived in a pool at Yamahiro in Japan; twice in every century it turned into a golden bird whose cry was like a wolf's howl, and which was an omen of impending famine and plague.   (463)

Oni   Japanese demons; basically human in appearance, they had claws, two horns and a malignant grimace; not unlike western devils, but without tails.   (463)

On Niont   A giant snake worshipped by the Huron Indians. It had a large sharp horn on its head, which could cut through mountains. It was never seen; nor could its home be discovered.   (488)

Onocentaur   Half-man, half-ass, this creature would starve itself to death if captured rather than lose its liberty. It was never known to sleep.

It seems to be a medieval variation on the CENTAUR.   (401)

Ophois   A warlike Egyptian wolf-god worshipped at Lykopolis (now Assiut).   (490)

Opinicus A heraldic variation of a griffin, with the body and four legs of a lion (a heraldic griffin has only two legs). It has the neck and wings of an eagle and a short camel's tail. Also called Epimacus. (515)

Orc Pliny says that this is an animal which is the particular enemy of the whale, but which can only be described as an 'enormous mass of flesh armed with teeth'. One was seen at Ostia under the Emperor Claudius, which gorged itself on a cargo of hides that had fallen overboard. It reappears in Ariosto's epic poem *Orlando Furioso* as the beast in a Perseus and Andromeda episode, with Rogero as Perseus and the fair Angelica as Andromeda.

> *Yet with his speare in hand, though not in rest,*
> *The ugly Orke upon the brow he strake,*
> *(I call him Orke, because I know no beast,*
> *Nor fish from whence comparison to take)*
> *His head and teeth were like a bore, the rest*
> *A masse, of which I know not what to make.*
> *He gave him on the brow a mighty knocke,*
> *But pierst no more then if it were a rocke.*

In the end Orlando slew it by placing an anchor in its mouth to prop its jaws open, and attacking it from within. Spenser compared his Blatant Beast to an orc. A still more recent incarnation is in Tolkien's *Lord of the Rings*, where orcs form part of the hosts of the Dark Lord of Mordor. Now the generic name of the killer-whale. (118, 303)

Oreads, *see* NYMPHS

Orthos Two-headed dog who guarded the OXEN OF GERYON; brother to CERBERUS.

Ovda Spirit resembling a man but with feet turned backwards and a naked hairy body, the terror of travellers in the Volga region. It could be heard laughing in the forest, and if it came across a traveller, it would tickle him to death, unless its victim touched it under its left armpit, where there was a hole; this rendered it powerless. It rode horses left out at pasture, racing them around the field until they were nearly dead. (482)

Oxen of Geryon   These cattle had three bodies, and were guarded by the giant Eurytion and the dog Orthos on the island of Erytheia. As one of his twelve tasks to win his bride Deianeira, Hercules had to slay the guardians and carry off the oxen, which he successfully accomplished.

(417)

Padfoot   A demon dog said to haunt the countryside near Leeds. (413)

Pajar   A bird which cherished its young and fed them well. The nestlings were ungrateful, however, and beat the parents with their wings. The pajar killed its young in anger, but at once repented. After three days of mourning, it opened its own breast and revived them with its own blood. It is another version, from Rumania, of medieval belief about the pelican.

(214)

Palesmurt   Found in the Volga region, this 'half-man' had only half a body, one eye, one foot, one hand and one breast; the latter was so huge that it suffocated unwary passers-by by pressing it in their mouths. It could be heard shrieking in the twilight. Compare NESNAS and DIREACH GHLINN EITIDH.

(482)

Pan   Originally the Greek God of the woods and fields, Pan became the symbol of the wild, feared at night (hence *panic*); and later he stood for the heathen way of life. His head, face and arms were human, but he was horned and had the belly and legs of a goat. Also known in a slightly different guise as Sylvanus; his followers were FAUNS or ICHTHYO-CENTAURS.

(417)

P'an Ku   The creator-giant in later Chinese myths. Originally a dwarf, he grew six feet each day during the creation, which lasted 18,000 years.

PARANDE

At the end of his task he died, and the various parts of his body became the wind, the mountains, the rivers and so on; the insects crawling over his body became human beings. Compare Ymir under GIANTS.   (518)

Pantheon   A heraldic panther, described in 1513 as 'a best lyke a woulf sable, full of sterres gold, . . . his fete cloven lyke a hogge'.   (474)

Panthera   Sir John Mandeville describes these creatures as having blood-red skins which shine against the sun; they are worth their weight in gold and are found in a great city named Cadon. They are presumably another version of the real panther.   (219)

Papillon   The magic fire-breathing horse of the fairy Morgana in Pulci's *Orlando Innamorato*.

Papstesel   According to a report to the Venetian government, this monster was found in the Tiber flood of January 1496. It had an ass's head on a woman's body; and one arm was an elephant's trunk, one leg that of an eagle, one that of an ox; on its back was the face of a bearded man, and there was a serpent's head on its tail. It was the subject of a satire on the Papacy in 1523 by Luther and Melanchthon, Luther christening it *Papstesel* or Papal ass, and taking it as a symbol of the Papacy's decay and corruption.   (465, 315)

Para   A cat-like spirit which collected for its owner milk, cream and butter, or sometimes money and grain. Anyone wishing to own one could fashion it out of stolen female garments with the head of a thread-ball and the foot made of a spindle. It was found in Finland and Sweden (Swedish Bjära) and in Lapland, where it is known as 'cream-cat' or Smierragatto.   (482)

Parande or **Parandrus**   An Ethiopian beast like an ibex with branching horns and a stag's head. Normally it was brown like a bear, but it could change colour to merge with its surroundings. It was timid and took to flight if frightened.   (118)

Peg Powler   A nixie (see NIX) found in the Tees; like others of her kind she had green hair and was insatiable for human life. The foam on the upper reaches of the river was called 'Peg Powler's suds'.   (413)

Pegasi   Horse-headed birds found in Scythia; Pliny, who reports their appearance, regards them as fabulous.   (118)

Pegasus   The winged horse of Greek myth, reputedly either a son of Poseidon or moulded from the drops of blood from the Medusa's head when Perseus flew off with his gruesome trophy. Bellerophon rode him when he slew the CHIMERA, but later tried to ride him to heaven, fell off at a great height and was killed. Pegasus was the symbol of inspiration; the fountain Hippocrene from which the poets drank on Mount Olympus was opened by a blow from his hoof.   (428)

Peist   Irish dragon imprisoned by St Patrick.

Peluda   A monster which terrorised La Ferté-Bernard in the middle ages. It had survived the flood without being taken into the Ark, and it had a serpent's head, a green spherical body covered in poisonous spines and turtle's feet. It breathed fire and plundered stables at night; when it was driven away by peasants it plunged into the river Huisne and flooded the district. It was finally slain by the fiancé of a maiden whom it had dragged off.

Pheng   A huge Japanese bird, not unlike a ROC, whose flight eclipsed the sun; it could swallow a camel whole, and its hollow quills were used as water casks.   (222)

Phillyloo Bird   American stork which flew upside down in order to keep warm and to avoid rheumatism. See FEARSOME CRITTERS. (412)

Phoenix   For a mythical creature the phoenix is familiar enough; it is used in everyday life as a trademark, it rises from stylised flames on heraldic bearings, it enriches the poet's language and appears briefly in history. What its legend is and means, on the other hand, has largely been forgotten as the symbol has gained wider and wider currency.

PHOENIX

The phoenix, according to the most developed forms of the story, is a bird about the size of an eagle, brilliantly coloured in plumage; it is either purple with a golden collar, or a dazzling mixture of red, gold and blue. It is the only one of its kind, and lives in Arabia; at the end of an epoch, as it feels death drawing near, it builds a pyre of the sweetest spices, on which it then sits singing a song of rare beauty. The rays of the sun ignite the nest, and both this and the bird are consumed to ashes. From the ashes there arises a worm, which grows in due course into a new phoenix. The bird's first task is to gather the remains of its parent, and accompanied by a throng of other birds, to fly to Heliopolis (the city of the Sun) on the Nile. Here the priests of the sun receive it with great ceremony; it buries its parent and returns to Arabia.

The roots of this story which lack the principal feature of the fiery death, first appear in ancient Greek literature, in Herodotus's account of Egypt (*c.* 430 B.C.). When he was at Heliopolis he was shown the bird in pictures; and its very name may be due to his confusing it with the date-palm on which it is often depicted, which is also *phoenix* in Greek. It was a red-gold bird about the size of an eagle, and the priests said that it arrived there every five hundred years bearing its predecessor embalmed in a ball of myrrh, which it buried in the temple of the sun. From later writers we glean details, such as the bird's rebirth as a worm from its dead parent's body and the accompanying flight of birds. There was, however, some doubt as to the length of the true interval between the arrival of two phoenixes: Aelain (*c.* A.D. 200) mocks the priests who do not know when it will arrive and 'have to confess that they devote their time "to putting the sun to rest with their talk", but do not know as much as birds'. Tacitus (*c.* A.D. 100) reports, 'Regarding the length of its life, accounts vary. The commonest view favours 500 years. But some estimate that it appears every 1461 years . . .' The particular phoenix which had come to his attention as a historian was that said to have arrived in the reign of Tiberius; but since the previous one had been welcomed at Heliopolis under Ptolemy III, and as between Ptolemy and Tiberius there were less than 250 years 'some have denied the authenticity of the Tiberian phoenix, which did not, they say, come from Arabia or perform the tra-ditionally attested actions'. Pliny rejects it out of hand; although it was displayed in public, 'nobody would doubt that this phoenix is a fabrica-tion'.

PHOENIX

It is only in the fourth century A.D. that the idea of a fiery death is to be found, in two complete poems on the phoenix, by Claudian and Lactantius. This description of the bird's death is taken from Claudian in Henry Vaughan the Silurist's translation:

> *He knows his time is out! and doth provide*
> *New principles of life; herbs he brings dried*
> *From the hot hills, and with rich spices frames*
> *A Pile shall burn, and Hatch him with his flames.*
> *On this the weakling sits; salutes the Sun*
> *With pleasant noise, and prays and begs for some*
> *Of his own fire, that quickly may restore*
> *The youth and vigour, which he had before.*
> *Whom soon as Phoebus spyes, stopping his rayns*
> *He makes a stand, and thus allayes his pains . . .*
> *He shakes his locks, and from his golden head,*
> *Shoots one bright beam, which smites with vital fire*
> *The willing bird; to burn is his desire,*
> *That he may live again; he's proud in death,*
> *And goes in haste to gain a better breath.*
> *The spicie heap fir'd with celestial rays*
> *Doth burn the aged Phoenix, when strait stays*
> *The chariot of th'amazed Moon; the pole*
> *Resists the wheeling, swift Orbs, and the whole*
> *Fabric of Nature at a stand remains,*
> *Till the old bird a new, young being gains.*

Where did such a tale come from, and are its details mere decoration or part of the clues as to its origin? Herodotus's account of the phoenix as a sacred bird at Heliopolis sets us in the right direction; for in the Egyptian mythological texts, such as the Book of the Dead, which are concerned with the soul's safety in the other world and are often magical and obscure, the bird *bn.w* or *bennu* appears, with many of the attributes of the phoenix. This creature is one of the prime movers of the world: prototype of the individual soul, it arises from the Isle of Fire in the underworld and flies to Heliopolis to announce the new epoch, in which the sun itself is renewed. Because the sun, too, had been envisaged as a bird which made its daily journey from east to west, so the bennu came to be identified with

Khepera himself, and a new idea of the bennu appears as a bird accompanying the sun on its daily journey. In the Apocalypse of Baruch (second century A.D.), Baruch is shown by an angel the sun as it sets out on its daily journey, accompanied by the phoenix 'a bird a large as nine mountains'; and at twilight, the same procession returns. The phoenix is weary, 'because he holds back the rays of the sun, because of the fire and heat which last throughout the day . . . if his wings did not form a screen against the rays of the sun, no living being would survive'. This legend reappears in a slightly different form in the story of the bird called heliodromos or sun-runner, and other variations linger in the medieval descriptions of the phoenix itself.

The bennu's colouring, gold, red, pink and blue, is that of the phoenix. Among the few details of its habits, we learn of the flight of birds which escorts it at a respectful distance, perhaps a simile for the stars following Venus at eventide. A sarcophagus bears the inscription 'I am the bennu who begets himself and gives incense to Osiris'. The identification with Osiris the god of resurrection, which is found elsewhere, strengthens the idea of the bennu as self-reviving. Finally the bennu is associated with the new epoch or great year in the same way as the phoenix. The cycle of 1461 days (Tacitus's 'years' is an error) is exactly the length of four solar years including leap year day. All in all, there can be little doubt that the phoenix of Herodotus and classical tradition is indeed the same creature as the bennu of Egyptian myth.

In the medieval Bestiaries variations developed, both orthodox and unorthodox; the phoenix is confused with the eagle in one version, but the most interesting is that of the bestiary of the heretical Waldensian sect. This revives an aspect of the legend which was rarely touched on: the phoenix's sweet song on its pyre, which was taken to symbolise man's duty of praising God. Although this story is very like that of the swan's song, it is a very old attribute of the phoenix, and found in Roman writers. In the most unusual of all the bestiaries, the *Lovers' Book of Beasts*, the phoenix masquerades as a salamander, and can only be identified by the illustration, which shows it as a bird; the same confusion also occurs in Arabian writers.

From theology, the phoenix migrates to literature. In the sixteenth century it was particularly used in poems about Elizabeth I, and also by Shakespeare in *The Phoenix and the Turtle*. The cold sceptical eye of the seventeenth century ejected it from the canon of natural history. Poets, on the other hand, seized on it as an exotic symbol of the unique – which quickly became debased to the merely rare – and phoenixes abound in their eulogies of monarchs and other great men of the world, and in the lines inspired by the great beauties of the day: in this century, Yeats, thinking of Maud Gonne, could revive the myth's magic as he scorned 'a score of duchesses surpassing womankind' for her sake, saying 'I knew a phoenix in my youth, so let them have their day'. Or Florian, the eighteenth-century French writer of fables, can give the myth a new charm by placing it in a homely setting. One day the phoenix appears in the forests of France, where all the birds are overcome with envy and admiration – all, that is, save the turtle-dove; she sighs as she gazes at the phoenix, and when her mate asks her the reason for this, answers: 'I can only pity him; he is the only one of his kind.' On a much more complex and subtle plane are three symbolic recreations of the legend in poems by D. H. Lawrence, Sidney Keyes and Herbert Read. In Keyes's poem, the phoenix stands for corrupting pride, while in sharp contrast Read sees it as archetype of life's continuation. We have come full circle: from the subtle religious myths of ancient Egypt to the equally subtle personal myths of modern poetry.

The phoenix may have its distant origin in the habit of anting with fire, which has been observed by Maurice Burton in a number of birds; the posture adopted during this performance (which provides some obscure kind of sensual stimulation) is strikingly like that of the phoenix in Egyptian art. See also FENG-HWANG (Chinese phoenix).

(118, 456, 424, 419)

Phooka, see POOKA

Phykis　A brightly coloured bird found in the Mediterranean. Fishermen bit it to death, but if it slipped down their throat, they died.　(431)

Piasa　In American Indian myths, 'the bird which devours men', portrayed in similar fashion to a Chinese dragon on the rocks at Alton, Illinois.　(436)

Picktree Brag　A Durham version of the BOGEY BEAST. Its usual forms were animal, but it sometimes appeared as a headless naked man.　(413)

Ping-Feng A Chinese creature with the body of a black pig, but with a human head at each end. (411)

Pontarf A monstrous fish found in the western seas of Europe, which carried off young children. (321)

Pooka A wild shaggy colt hung with chains which haunted wild places, and misled benighted travellers. Related in its mischievous habits to the English Puck which has become a household spirit: also called Phooka, Welsh Pwca. (413)

Portunes Gervase of Tilbury in the twelfth century reported that these creatures went about English farmhouses in hoops. They were dwarf-like, with tiny wrinkled faces, and well disposed to men; their only form of mischief was to mislead horsemen. (211)

Prion 'This beast has long wings, and when it sees a ship sailing, it raises its wings on high and sails, wagering jealously with the ship. Yet, when it has made but twenty or thirty stadia, it grows tired and folds its wings . . .' so a medieval sailor must have once described a flying-fish to an inquiring monk. (204)

Prock Gwinter, see GUYASCUTUS

Puk A small household dragon, represented as a four-footed serpent about eighteen inches long which brings treasure to its master. In its earliest form it was probably a household-spirit from Germany (compare Puck in England), but it became part of Baltic folklore when German colonists moved into that area in the Middle Ages. It is the same as the Lithuanian AITVARAS or kaukas, or the Estonian tulihänd. (470)

Pwca, see POOKA

Pyong The Chinese equivalent of the ROC.

Pyragones, pyrallis or **pyrausta** 'In the copper smelting furnaces of Cyprus, in the very midst of the fire, there is to be seen flying about a four-footed animal with wings, the size of a large fly . . . So long as it remains in the fire it will live, but if it comes out and flies a little distance from it, it will die instantly.' – Pliny. (118)

Qiqion   A huge hairless dog which is feared by the Eskimos because when it approached men or dogs, they are seized with fits. But it is a timid and stupid creature, and can be frightened off by mentioning its name. It has hair only on its mouth, feet, ears and tip of the tail. (470)

Questing Beast   A beast pursued by Sir Palomides in Arthurian romance. Malory describes it as serpent-headed, with the body of a lybard, 'buttokked like a lyon and footed like an harte. And in hys body there was such a noyse as hit had bene twenty couple of hounds questynge, and suche noyse that beste made wheresomever he wente.' Questing originally meant the barking of hounds as they found the scent. Malory continues, with a play on the word: 'And this beste evermore Sir Palomydes followed, for hit was called hys queste.' It reappears in the *Faerie Queene* as the thousand-tongued Blatant Beast, the spirit of calumny and courtiers' gossip, which Spenser feared as the enemy of his own poems. In T. H. White's *The Once and Future King*, the beast is pursued by King Pellinore, an elderly and gently comic figure, who is just as liable to wrap the beast in his best overcoat as actually to pursue it. (317, 457)

Quetzalcoatl   'Green Feather-Snake', in Aztec myth, god of the rain-bearing trade wind, who later became god of the four elements. He was usually represented as a benevolent old man driven from the kingdom by evil magicians. He departed over the eastern sea, but was expected to return; hence the invading Spaniards were mistaken for him. As the god of wind, he became the 'breath of life', and hence the creative force. (508)

Rabican   The horse of Astolpho in Ariosto's *Orlando Furioso* born of

> *a close union of the wind and flame*
> *And, nourished not by hay or heartening corn,*
> *Fed on pure air . . .*

Astolpho abandoned him for the HIPPOGRIFF, but later returned to him.

(303)

Râhu, *see* ALICHA

Raiden   Japanese thunder-god, shown as a demon or ONI with two claws on each foot; he carried a drum on his back. In storms he jumped from tree to tree and preyed on men's navels. A mosquito net and the burning of incense were the only means of protection against him, though the peasants often lay on their stomachs during storms to protect their navels.

Raksasas   Men with red hair and eyes, of demonic appearance, with a mouth stretching from one spear-pointed ear to the other. They could change shape at will, appearing as beautiful girls if they wished. They preyed on pilgrims and travellers in wild places, devouring either them or the sacrifices offered by them.

(484)

Ram-Eagle   A compound heraldic beast.

Ratatosk, *see* NIDHOGG

Rath   A kind of turtle with a shark's mouth, an erect head, and forelegs so curved that it walked on its knees. Its diet, according to Lewis Carroll, consisted of oysters; perhaps it deserved to be mistaken for a kind of green pig.

Rawhead A pond spirit or NIX found in Northern England, also known as Bloody Bones; it dragged children into its lair and drowned them. It was this spirit, recorded as early as the fifteenth century, which gave its name to the pirate flag of skull and crossbones (otherwise the Jolly Roger). (413)

Redcap A malignant spirit in the shape of a squat old man with long nails and a red cap dyed in blood which haunted the peel towers along the Scottish border. It attacked humans, but could be driven off by quoting the Bible or by the sight of the cross in the shape of a sword-handle. The redcap at Grandtully Castle, Perthshire was of a different kind, and was regarded as lucky. (413)

Reem A wild ox of immense size, so vast that it could be mistaken for a mountain. Only two of the species existed; they inhabited the far east and the far west, and met once every seventy years to mate, after which they died, the female having given birth to male and female twins. The Hebrew myths tell how Noah tied them to the stern of the ark to save them from the flood. They were perhaps a dim memory of a species of bison or even of the aurochs. The mistranslation of *reem* as unicorn accounts for the appearance of the latter in the Authorised Version. (444)

Remora *Let all the winds in one Winde gather them*
And (seconded with Neptunes strongest stream)
Let all at once blow all their stiffest gales
A-stern in a Galley under all her sails;
Let her be holpen with a hundred Owers,
Each lively handled by five lusty Rowers:
The Remora, fixing her feeble horn
Into the tempest-beaten Vessels stern,
Stayes her stone-still, while all her stout Consorts
Saile thence at pleasure to their wished Ports.
    Joshua Sylvester, *Du Bartas his divine weekes and Workes.*

The remora was a minute creature a foot long and four inches thick, which wrapped its tail round a rock and with its mouth or a horn attached itself to the vessel. With its power of suction, it was supposed to draw up sunken gold, while it was also said to have held back Antony's flagship at the battle of Actium. It is akin to the real remora or sucking-fish, but endowed with mythical powers. (307)

Ricaboo Racker, *see* GUYASCUTUS

Rigi, *see* AREOP-ENAP

Rinjin   The Japanese dragon-king, dwelling in a palace under the sea. For dragon-kings, see DRAGON. (463)

Roc, or **Rukh** (Chinese **Pyong**)   An immense bird which fed on young elephants, in shape like an eagle, though some accounts said that it was half-lion and half-bird. Its existence was generally believed in throughout the East, but it became confused with GRIFFINS and GARUDA BIRDS. The ANGKA is the Arabic equivalent; the rook in chess derives its name from the roc. Marco Polo reported them from Madagascar, and

said that one had been known to carry off a bride in her bridal array. The adventures of Sinbad include a similar episode: Sinbad landed on a desert island, on which there was nothing except a vast white cupola. On the next day a cloud obscured the sun. The cupola was a roc's egg, the shadow that of the roc. Sinbad climbed onto its foot and was carried off to a high mountain without the roc noticing.

The giant *Aepyornis* of Madagascar, whose thirteen-inch high eggs held about two gallons, and which stood eight or nine feet high, is probably at the root of these stories, suitably exaggerated by travellers. (221, 453)

Rocking-Horse Fly   Made entirely of wood, this creature moved through Looking Glass forests by swinging itself from branch to branch. It lived off a diet of sap and sawdust, according to Lewis Carroll.

Rompo   A creature found in India and Africa which fed on dead men; it had a long slender body and tail, with a hare's head and mouth, man's ears, badger's feet in front and bear's feet behind, and a mane. It is another description of the hyena, which, being nocturnal and shy, was difficult to identify accurately.   (458)

Roperite   An animal with a long flexible beak which it used to rope rabbits, occasionally capturing a raw lumberjack instead. It was the size of a wild horse and travelled in herds. (See FEARSOME CRITTERS.)
(412)

Rosualt   Another name for MURRISK.

Rumptifusel   A large and bellicose beast which slept by wrapping its body round a tree. As it was thin and furry, passing lumberjacks were known to make the fatal error of mistaking it for a fur coat. (See FEAR-SOME CRITTERS.)   (412)

Saehrimnir   (The 'Blackened'.) The magic boar which was cooked each night in Valhalla (the Norse heaven), and served to the assembled warriors, but which revived to be hunted and eaten again the next day.

Safat A creature of the upper atmosphere, flying out of sight of the naked eye; it was dragon-headed. (477)

Sahab Described by Olaus Magnus in the sixteenth century as a sea-beast with small cow's feet and a large body found off the Norwegian coast. One long foot was used as a hand for feeding and for self-defence. It was amphibious, breathing in in the water and out in the air. It could also spout like a whale. (316)

Saint Attracta's Monster An Irish beast which roared like a lion, had boar's tusks, fiery eyes and ram's ears. The saint made the sign of the cross over him with her staff and he fell dead. (430)

Saint Senan's Monster A creature which lived on the island of Iniscathy, banished by St Senan. It was amphibious with a horse's mane, fiery breath, a belly like a bellows and a whale's tail. A single eye gleamed in its forehead, and it struck fire from the rocks with its iron nails. (430)

Salamander The real salamander is a small lizard with no particularly remarkable properties. In classical nature lore, however, its original

peculiarity was that it could extinguish fire by walking through it, by virtue of its coldness. Aristotle quoted it as an example of an animal which fire did not harm, when discussing the pyrallis (see PYRAGONES); but the properties of the pyrallis were later attributed to the salamander, so that it was reputed to live *in* the fire. Aelian says that it lives particularly in forges, and if it is being helpful the forge gives no trouble. If the fire goes out and the bellows blow in vain, the smiths know that it is working against them. 'Accordingly they track it down and exact vengeance; and then the fire is lit up, is easily coaxed up, and does not go out.' It was later supposed to be nourished by fire, and asbestos was said to be salamander's wool. The accounts which give it highly poisonous teeth or the power of poisoning trees or water are part of a more general medieval belief that lizards were poisonous. (104, 118, 499)

Sarabha When Vishnu took the form of a NARASINHA, he so frightened the lesser gods that they prayed to Siva to deal with him. Siva thereupon took the shape of a Sarabha, which was fiercer and stronger than the lion, and Vishnu was discomfited.

Sargon Amphibious fish which lusted after she-goats when it went ashore. Fishermen caught it by covering themselves in goat skins. It was the emblem of adultery and had goat's horns, 'for those that make horns on other men's heads do but make engines to tosse themselves to hell'. (321)

Sasabonsam A tall being with long legs and feet pointing both ways, which lived in the Gold Coast forests. It was hairy and had bloodshot eyes; and it lurked in trees, hooking up passing Ashanti hunters with its feet.

Satyrs Attendants of Bacchus (Dionysos) and PAN, they were very like Pan in appearance, with the legs and hindquarters of a goat, small horns and goat-like ears. Anatolian satyrs were reputed to have horse's ears, feet and tail. Monkeys and apes were frequently classified as satyrs in the Middle Ages; Bartholomew Anglicus distinguished seven kinds, including the CYCLOPS and SCIAPODS as well as two with large ears or lips, and one curious variety without mouths, which breathed through a hole in their breast. Satyrs proper were nearer to the medieval wild men or WODEWOSES, or to the medieval devil, though their only vice was immoderate lust and drunkenness, venial rather than mortal sins. (228)

Satyral   An Indian version of the MANTICHORA or man-tiger.   (515)

Satyre-Fish, Winged   A compound heraldic monster with satyr's head, fish body and wings.   (476)

Schrat   Wild and shaggy German male wood-spirit, which could be a form of nightmare spirit. It could be recognised by its eyebrows, which met in the middle. See also WODEWOSES and WOODWIVES.

Sciapods   Men with one foot so large that they could lie on their back and use it as a sunshade. They were usually described as one legged, and very swift, though a four-legged species which used one leg as shelter

while walking is also reported. They lived on the fragrance of fruit only, and carried fruit with them when they travelled for this purpose; if they breathed corrupt air they died. Also called Monoscelans.   (119, 450)

Scitalis   A snake which was a very sluggish crawler, and therefore hypnotised its prey by the splendour of its skin; according to medieval lore men were fascinated by its beauty and it was then able to catch them easily.   (228)

Scolopendra   The largest of all sea-monsters. It floats with its head above water, and long bristles come out of its nostrils; its tail is flat, like a crayfish, and it 'rows' with numerous feet down each side of its body like a trireme. If it swallows bait and is hooked, it will regurgitate its stomach, extract the hook and swallow it again. Bernard Heuvelmans in *In the Wake of the Sea-Serpents* relates it to the type of sea-serpent seen by the French navy off Vietnam, which he classifies as the Many-Finned Sea-Serpent. (101, 321, 454)

Scylla   The fearsome monster of the Odyssey was originally a water-nymph whom Glaucus wooed, pretending to be a god in disguise. Scylla spurned him, whereupon Glaucus enlisted Circe's aid. Circe fell in love with him herself, and out of jealousy poisoned the water where Scylla bathed so that it swarmed with serpents. These became part of her, and she took to devouring mariners. Another version ascribes her transformation to Amphitrite, and says that she was six-headed. Her shape is somewhat reminiscent of that of a giant squid. The straits where she was supposed to dwell were probably the Straits of Messina between Italy and Sicily. (115)

Scythian Ass   Related to the unicorn, this beast seems to have been merged with the former after a few early reports in Greek sources. Its horn, like that of the unicorn, was a powerful antidote to poison, and was the only vessel which could contain the infernal waters of the river Styx. (431)

Sea Mouse   A mouse which laid eggs in a hole which it then covered with earth. When the young were born, they were blind, and the mother took them to the sea, where they lost their blindness. (405)

Sea-Serpent   Regarded by most scientists as definitely fabulous in the mid-nineteenth century, this creature is now almost respectable. In 1875 a captain who had seen and reported a sea-serpent said that the writer of one letter had replied 'that she pitied anyone that was related to anyone that had seen the sea-serpent,' a reaction that was fairly usual despite well-documented accounts from naval officers which had been printed in the *Illustrated London News*, and an increasing number of well-attested sightings. One of the problems was that the creature appeared to have a method of locomotion – the famous undulating humps – unlike any other known fish or reptile, and which seemed theoretically impossible from a mechanical point of view; and, to further confuse the issue, very few reliable witnesses described the beast in the same terms. Besides the humped species, there were smooth eel-like examples, long-necked specimens, and giant squids (or pieces of them). So the genus sea-serpent came to include everything from LEVIATHAN to KRAKEN as well, meaning generally any large unidentified sea-creature. Assorted washed-up remains extended the range of possibilities, particularly when examined by amateurs who could only report what they saw and could not relate it to what the creature had looked like when alive. The showmen cashed in as well, manufacturing serpents from perfectly genuine fossils; and as a result all sea-serpents were tarred with the same brush, as a kind of Victorian equivalent of a flying saucer.

Gradually the evidence has been sifted into some kind of order, and the false trails discarded: the almost skeletal remains of basking sharks and eels have been properly identified, the fantastic or attention-seeking reports discredited, the fossils put into their proper relationship, and a small core of solid evidence established. The giant squid, the original of the KRAKEN, has been accepted by science. Of the sea-serpent proper, according to Bernard Heuvelman's recent investigation, there are six main types: the long-necked, the many-humped, the many-finned, the merhorse, the super-otter and the super-eel. He also distinguishes three lesser types. It is at first sight a little difficult to accept that we must believe in the existence of *nine* species where only one was considered incredible a little while ago, but between twelve and forty-eight sightings are recorded for each of his main types, and this does go a long way to explain the extraordinary variety of the sea-serpent's reported appearance.

Not the least curious point about the sea-serpent is that if it is fabulous, it is a comparatively recent fabulous beast. Most of the curiosities of classical natural history, distorted by medieval writers who were not interested in scientific accuracy, can now be explained either as real phenomena or as pictorial evidence in a foreign country which has been misunderstood (cf PHOENIX and UNICORN); other creatures from this period and from other continents can be explained in terms of symbols, and belong to the imagery of religion. But the sea-serpent does not appear in classical times, except as a general sea-monster, nor has he the least religious significance. Many of the sightings are such as to demand an explanation in keeping with the rational and factual description of what was seen: and though unskilled observers can make mistakes, there is still the idea of a huge marine serpent to be accounted for, an idea which is either a piece of semi-scientific folklore invented in an age which prided itself on being rational, and for that reason unusual enough, or which has its basis in reality. (316, 454)

Sedus and **Lamassus** Winged bulls and cows with human heads from Assyrian carvings. They were usually good spirits who guarded doorways: there is a very fine one from a gateway at Nineveh in the British Museum. The good sedus turned away evil; but their wicked counterparts were a kind of spirit-demon. (484)

Sekamet The Egyptian goddess Hathor as the spirit of war: represented as a lion-headed woman wading in blood. (490)

Semuru or **Senmurv,** *see* SIMURGH

Serpent, Flying The flying serpent of Isa was hatched from a cockatrice's egg, and was the most deadly of all creatures. It appears in the Old Testament as a symbol for power. (514)

Serpent, Horned A rain god of the Pueblo Indians, dwelling either in the sky or in water. It was the enemy of the THUNDERBIRD. (436)

Serpent, Winged Among the Algonquin Indians this creature had a man's face, a tiger's beard and a fish's tail. It was probably originally a rain god. Marco Polo also reports seven-headed winged tree serpents which can kill a man with their breath. (436, 222)

Serra A winged sea-monster with a lion's head and fish's tail. When it saw a ship, it caught the wind in its wings and sailed towards the ship, until it could not go any further, when it folded its wings and sank back into the sea. It was reputed to sink ships frequently, though the method it used is not recorded. Cf. PRION, also a garbled report of a flying-fish. (214)

Sesha World serpent, king of the NĀGĀS, in Hindu myth. He had a thousand heads, and was shown dressed in purple, holding a plough and a pestle. He supported the world, and earthquakes were caused by him shaking one of his heads; Vishnu rested on him when sleeping. He destroyed the world by fire at the end of every cycle of a thousand ages. Cf VARAHA.   (470)

Sevienda Nicolo d'Conti described this Indian version of the PHOE-NIX, which burnt itself to death on a nest of dry wood, singing sweetly. From the ashes came a worm which developed into a bird like its progenitor. It was distinguished by its curious beak, which was full of holes.   (223)

Shagamaw Beast with hind-legs of moose and fore-legs of bear, using each pair alternately to baffle trackers. It devoured any clothing which lumbermen left around when logging, but its fierce appearance hid a gentle and shy nature. See FEARSOME CRITTERS.   (412)

Shahapet 'Serpent-ghost' which appeared as both man and serpent, found in India, where it was the guardian of particular places. It was driven out of the homesteads into the fields in March in order to ensure a good harvest, and brought good fortune to the house at other times. Because it might appear as a stranger seeking shelter, travellers could not be turned away.   (484)

Shmoo Probably the only fabulous creature which originated in a comic strip and had a whole book written about its demise. Al Capp invented this all-providing animal in his 'Li'l Abner' strip; it was a ham-shaped, tasty-looking beast with a rapturous smile permanently in place, which ate nothing and multiplied rapidly. It was delicious to eat, and if looked at hungrily would drop dead of sheer pleasure. It laid fresh eggs, butter and milk, and its flesh tasted of steak when grilled, boneless chicken when boiled or fried. Its eyes could be used as suspender buttons, and its hide produced the finest leather. Its appearance in Dogpatch, the scene of Li'l Abner's adventures, solved the inflation problem there, and so disturbed the capitalist economy that it had to be killed off. Capp was accused of 'Shmoocialism', and later wrote a book about the episode. It differs from other fabulous creatures of the comic world in that it has no anthropomorphic traits, and is purely an invented *beast*.   (470)

Shony   A Cornish ghost-dog whose appearance heralded a storm. (459)

Shriker   Said in the North Country to be an invisible creature which shrieked in the woods, as a portent of death; when it did appear, it had huge feet and saucer eyes. Otherwise called a brash from the noise of its padding feet.   (413)

Shrovetide Bear (Fastnachtsbär)   A man or boy dressed realistically in bearskins went round the houses of South German villages at Shrovetide, dancing with the womenfolk. He was given money (which he and his companions later spent on drinking) as his reward for performing this fertility rite. Cf OATS GOAT.   (470)

Shuck   Dog-like creature about the size of a calf or a donkey, sometimes white but usually black with fiery eyes, found on East Anglia coasts; a terrifying and unwelcome apparition.   (513)

Side   The fairy race of Ireland, often called *Tuatha dé Danaan*, who dwelt in barrows. Cf BARROW-WIGHTS for a more fearsome memory of the Bronze Age peoples.   (470)

Sidehill Dodger, Sidehill Ganger, Sidewinder, *see* GUYASCUTUS

Simurgh, Semuru or **Senmurv**   Persian bird which sat on the tree of seeds near the tree of immortality, on which the seeds produced by all wild plants during the year were gathered. Its open wings were like a mist over the mountains, and when it alighted the seeds of the tree fell to the ground. Its feathers had magic properties, and would cure wounds, while the bird itself was the deadly enemy of snakes, like the garuda; and it lived behind veils of light and dark on inaccessible peaks in the Caucasus. Other reports gave it phoenix-like habits: it lived 1700 years and when the young were hatched the parent of the opposite sex burned itself to death. A thirteenth-century poem describes how the other birds decided to seek the simurgh so that he could settle their quarrels; after many hardships only thirty survived to find him (whose name meant thirty) and they realised that they themselves were the simurgh, purified by the

SIRENS

labour of their journey. Another story, from Kashmir, tells how a king
caught a simurgh which refused to sing. His wife reminded him that
simurghs only sang when they saw others of the same species, so he
deceived it by putting a mirror in its cage; at which it sang a sad melody
and died. In early accounts it is a griffin-like creature, half-dog and half-
bird, connecting sky and earth. In Arabic it is called ANGKA. See also
CHAMROSH, GARUDA, GRIFFIN, ROC, PHOENIX. (222, 477, 478)

Sirens (1) Originally river goddesses, they resisted the power of love
and were transformed by Aphrodite into half-birds, half-women. They
were already renowned for their singing, and after their transformation

dared to challenge the Muses to a singing contest. The Muses defeated
them and plucked out their wing-feathers; and the sirens fled to a
deserted islet off Southern Italy, where Odysseus, having just left Circe's

135

island, heard them. Circe had warned him of their charms, and he had himself lashed to the mast and his companions' ears stopped with wax. Any less prudent sailor who succumbed to their music was devoured by them. They could also be heard singing in storms, but were silent in fine weather. Another version of the myth attributed their origin to the drops of blood which fell from ACHELOUS' horn when it was torn off by Hercules. (109)

(2) Winged serpents found in Arabia who could fly as fast as a galloping horse, and whose bite was deadly. (216)

Sirrush or **Mushrush** Scaly creature with long neck and tail, serpent's head and tongue. Its fore-feet were like a cat's, its hind-feet like a bird's. It is depicted on the Ishtar gate at Babylon. (473)

Sisiutl Double-headed snake, which, according to the Pacific Coast Indians, could change into a fish. Its flesh was poisonous, but pieces of its body were used by medicine-men: the skin was so hard a knife would not pierce it, but it could be cut with a holly-leaf. (488)

Skinfaxi and **Hrimfaxi** In Scandinavian myth, Skinfaxi, 'shining-mane', and Hrimfaxi, 'frosty-mane', were the horses which brought day and night respectively. Hrimfaxi's foam gave dew to the earth each morning as he ended his course: Skinfaxi illuminated earth and heaven with his mane. (480)

Skoffin A basilisk-like creature found in Iceland, whose glance was deadly. Only the glance of another skoffin (which would kill both creatures), or a gun loaded with a silver button on which the sign of the cross was engraved, could destroy this monster. (418)

Sleipnir The eight-legged horse on which Odin rode, and which could overcome any obstacle in his path. (438)

Slidringtanni, see GULLINBURSTI

Sliver Cat A tree-cat found in the pine-woods of America, whose eyes were red, vertical slits. It had a long tail with a very hard knob on the end, one side of which was smooth, the other spiked. It lurked on a branch waiting for a lumberjack to pass underneath, when it knocked him down with the smooth side, and picked him up with the spikes. See FEARSOME CRITTERS. (412)

Smierragatto, *see* PARA

Snap-Dragon-Fly With wings of holly-leaves, a body of plum-pudding, and head of a raisin burning in brandy, this curious invention of Lewis Carroll's owes its form to a Victorian Christmas game of plucking raisins from a flaming dish. It lived off mince pies and nested in Christmas boxes.

Snark In Lewis Carroll's famous *The Hunting of the Snark* the Bellman gives these aids to snark recognition for the benefit of his companions:

> *'The first is the taste*
> *Which is meagre and hollow, but crisp:*
> *Like a coat that is rather too tight in the waist,*
> *With a flavour of Will-o'-the-wisp.*
>
> *Its habit of getting up late, you'll agree*
> *That it carries too far, when I say*
> *That it frequently breakfasts at five-o'clock tea,*
> *And dines on the following day.*
>
> *The third is its slowness in taking a jest,*
> *Should you happen to venture on one,*
> *It will sigh like a thing that is deeply distressed:*
> *And it always looks grave at a pun.*
>
> *The fourth is its fondness for bathing-machines,*
> *Which it constantly carries about,*
> *And believes that they add to the beauty of scenes—*
> *A sentiment open to doubt.*
>
> *The fifth is ambition. It next will be right*
> *To describe each particular batch:*
> *Distinguishing those that have feathers, and bite,*
> *From those that have whiskers and scratch.'*

BOOJUMS only were fatal; other varieties could be caught, taken home and served up with greens, their hide being useful for striking matches, though methods of trapping them were various, as the Bellman explained:

> '*You may seek it with thimbles—and seek it with care;*
> *You may hunt it with forks and hope;*
> *You may threaten its life with a railway-share;*
> *You may charm it with smiles and soap—.*'

Alas, the snark encountered by the expedition, and which the Baker attacked, proved to be the dreaded Boojum.

Sooner-Dog An American hound so bellicose it would sooner fight than eat.
(492)

Sphinx The great sphinx at Gizeh represents Horus, an incarnation of the sky or sun god; but another sphinx-like creature was the god of

wisdom, Hu. Egyptian sphinxes were strictly speaking male and symbols of royalty; the female sphinx is the emblem of the Babylonian moon-goddess, Astarte. Both kinds are shown with a human head and breast, the body, feet and tail of a lion, and bird's wings. The Greek sphinx, offspring of the monsters TYPHON and ECHIDNE was female, and infested the highroad near Thebes. Travellers who could not answer her riddle were devoured, until Oedipus found the correct answer. The sphinx asked: 'What is it, which, having but one voice, is first four-footed, then two-footed, and is at last three-footed', and Oedipus replied: 'The creature is man, for in infancy he crawls on all fours, in mature years he walks upright on two feet, and in old age goes as it were on three by the aid of a cane.' Hearing this, the sphinx threw herself off a cliff and was killed. (479, 490)

Splinter Cat An American animal which fed on wild bees and raccoons, which it extracted by charging at hollow trees and smashing them with its hard forehead. The result was similar to lightning or storm damage, and the work of hungry splinter cats was often attributed to these causes. See FEARSOME CRITTERS. (412)

Spriggan Ghosts of giants which haunted all megaliths and standing stones, guarding the treasure buried there. They could swell to a vast grotesque shape or shrink to a small size; and they were to blame for all kinds of disasters, such as falling buildings, bad weather or lost children. (413)

Squonk A shy beast, found in the hemlock forests of Pennsylvania. Its shyness was due to its appearance, for its loose skin was covered in warts and moles, and it wept continuously out of self-pity. It could be tracked by the trail of tears it left, but when frightened or captured was liable to dissolve entirely, leaving only tears and bubbles. See FEARSOME CRITTERS. (412)

Srvara Venomous yellow dragon slain by the hero Keresaspa in Armenian myth. Its teeth were as long as a man's arm, its ears as large as fourteen blankets and its horn as high as a mountain. (484)

Ssu Ling The four Spiritual Animals of China: the unicorn, or CH'I-LIN, head of all quadrupeds; the phoenix, or FENG-HWANG, chief of birds; the tortoise, of creatures with shells; the DRAGON, of all scaly animals. (486)

Stag, Celestial, *see* BUCCAS

Stellione   A lizard covered with stars and with a weasel's head, found in heraldry.   (515)

Stringes   A kind of Greek vampire which brought evil dreams and sucked the blood of sleepers.   (479)

Stymphalian Birds   Birds the size of cranes with brazen claws and beaks which dwelt in the marshes of lake Stymphalus in Arcadia. Hercules' fourth labour was to destroy them, which he did by frightening them with a magic rattle given to him by Athene and shooting them as they flew off. They seemed to have personified marsh fever.   (116)

Su   A creature from Patagonia, very violent and cruel. It was trapped by digging pits and camouflaging them. It carried its young on its back, but

always destroyed them before the hunter could reach them. It is probably the giant anteater, or even the giant sloth, redrawn from an early traveller's report.   (308, 453)

Sumargh, *see* SIMURGH

Swamfisck   A Norwegian fish which devoured other fish gluttonously. It protected itself by covering its head with skin and appearing to be dead fish or a lump of fat: but it stayed like this for so long that it had to eat its own flesh in order to survive.   (316)

Takujui   Like the Chinese CH'I-LIN, this Japanese creature only appeared when the reigning monarch was virtuous. In appearance it was similar to the KUDAN.   (463)

Talos   Man of bronze, last of the sons of the old gods of Greece, who guarded Crete. In order to enable Jason to land there, Medea enchanted him and grazed his ankle where there was a vulnerable exposed vein, and made him bleed to death.   (103)

Tanuki   Japanese badger spirit responsible for the growth of the rice crop, also called a wind-badger. If a wind-badger was killed and the wind blew, it was a sign that the creature had revived.   (477)

T'ao-Tieh, *see* KIRTIMUKHA

Tarandrus   Animal the size of an ox with horns and cloven hooves, found in Scythia. Its hair was as long as that of a bear, and its normal colour was that of an ass. But when the tarandrus was frightened, according to Aelian, it 'reflects the colour of all the trees, shrubs, and flowers or of the spots in which it is concealed; for this reason it is very rarely captured. It is wonderful that such various hues should be given to the body, but still more so that it should be given to the hair.'   (101)

Tarasque   According to the apocryphal life of St Martha, this dragon lived on the banks of the Rhone. It was bigger than an ox, larger than a horse, with a lion's head and mouth; its jaws contained vast teeth, it had six bear's paws, a carapace studded with spikes and a viper's tail. It was the offspring of LEVIATHAN and a BONNACON, and had come from Galatia in Asia Minor; and it made itself a public nuisance by attacking all passers-by on the banks or on the river until St Martha put a stop to its activities by drenching it with holy water just as it was occupied in devouring a man. It then became tame, but the local inhabitants did not trust it and killed it. Its demise is celebrated by a great fête at Whitsun, held at irregular intervals since the middle ages, in which the central feature is a huge effigy of the Tarasque, gaily decorated and with a movable head which spits fireworks into the crowds. There are many parallel episodes in Provençal myth, involving among others of the heavenly hierarchy, St Victor, St Andrew, St Armontaire and St Arletan. (434)

Tatsu Japanese dragon, similar to the DRAGON of China, but with three claws instead of five on each foot. (463)

Teakettler Small animal which made a noise like a boiling kettle. It preferred to walk backwards, with clouds of steam coming out of its nostrils. One of the rarer FEARSOME CRITTERS. (412)

Tengu Winged inhabitants of Japanese forests; the Konoha Tengu were semi-human with the wings and claws of giant eagles, while the Karasu Tengu were entirely birdlike. They were born from gigantic eggs and were evil and troublesome; wicked priests were believed to become tengu. However, government officials felt that a notice would control them, like ordinary inhabitants of Japan: the following was posted near the Nikko tombs in 1860:
  'To the Tengu and other Demons
  Whereas our Shogun intends to visit the Nikko Tombs next April, now therefore ye Tengu and other demons inhabiting these mountains must remove elsewhere until the Shogun's visit is concluded.
Mizuno, Lord of Dewa.' (463, 478)

Terrobuli Stones found in an Eastern mountain, which had male and female properties. When the pair were parted, they grew cool, but together they emitted fire. Medieval churchmen found them a useful illustration for their sermons on the dangers of carnal love. (404)

Thunderbirds All American Indian myths associate thunder with birds, and the belief is also found in Asia. The thunderbird haunted the realm of winds and clouds immediately above the earth, and was an invisible spirit. The lightning was the flashing of his eye, the thunder the noise of his wings. There were also lesser thunderbirds, such as the golden eagle. Mountain Indians believed the thunderbird to be a small red bird, which shot lightning arrows from its wing, the thunder being its wing rebounding. For the Pacific Indians it was a vast creature with a lake on its back from which the rain came; it ate whales and left their bones on top of mountains. (470, 488)

Tiamat The she-dragon of the ocean, which with Apsu, the sea of fresh-water, was one of the two beings at the beginning of creation in Sumerian myth. Marduk fought Tiamat in the *Epic of Creation*, a story which later appeared as Bel and the Dragon in the Apocrypha. In order to attack him, Tiamat created a host of monsters, which with her eleven dragons, accompanied her into battle against him. However, Marduk enmeshed her in a great net, and slew her with the help of the winds, which blew into her and tore her apart. As the first stage in the creation, her skin was stretched out to form the canopy of heaven. (436)

Ti-Chiang A Chinese bird found in the Celestial mountains: it was bright red, with six feet and four wings, but lacked face and eyes. (411)

T'ien Kou Sirius, the dog-star, was called T'ien Kou, the dog of heaven, by the Chinese; it portended destruction and catastrophe when it descended from the skies. (477)

Tityron or **Tityrus** Heraldic beast which is a cross between a sheep and a goat; sometimes called MUSIMON. (439)

Tlaloc, *see* CHAC

Tove Lewis Carroll describes it as a creature which nested under sundials; in appearance like a smooth white badger, with short stag's horns and long hind-legs, it had a tail like a corkscrew; its diet consisted chiefly of cheese.

Tragopan According to Pliny's rather doubting report, a bird bigger than an eagle found in Ethiopia. Its head was armed with ram's horns, and had purple plumage, the rest being brown. Otherwise called a *goteface*: perhaps an exaggerated account of the horned pheasant of which it is the generic name. (118, 119)

Tripoderoo Animal with two telescopic legs and a kangaroo's tail found in California. Its body was small, with a large snout. It crawled through the bush until it sighted its prey, when it extended its legs and fired a pellet of clay which it carried like a quid of tobacco in its cheek, using its snout in order to aim. See FEARSOME CRITTERS. (412)

Tritons Creatures with thick matted hair on their heads and scales on the rest of their body; they had a human nose but their mouths were wider, with big canine teeth, and they had gills under their ears. Their tails were like those of dolphins. They were the traditional attendants of

Neptune, blowing conch-shells, and can be found as decorations on many early maps. In classical times, specimens were to be seen at Tanagra and Rome, which, like other mermen, were probably JENNY HANIVERS. (101, 116)

Trolls Originally gigantic, demoniac beings in Scandinavian myth, the word was used to describe all kinds of monsters, for example Grendel. They were later confused with fairies and elves, of which they remain a larger version. They could bewitch men, including priests, but the sound of church bells drove them away. Night trolls who were still afoot at dawn were turned to stone, and standing stones were pointed out as petrified trolls. (427)

Tsuchi-gumo A giant earth spider which plagued a Japanese province in mythical times. It could not be harmed by steel and was finally killed by being trapped in a cave whose mouth was stopped by a metal net, and being smoked to death. (463)

Tulihänd, *see* PUK

Twrch Trywth A boar who had once been a king, but had been transformed by God as a punishment: the comb and shears which he carried between his ears were needed so that the giant Ysbaddaden could prepare himself for the wedding of his daughter Olwen to the hero Culhwch. Arthur, accompanied by his warriors and Mabon mab Modron and Gwyn ap Nudd as huntsmen, pursued it across Ireland, Wales and Cornwall. It finally disappeared into the sea off the Cornish coast, but the comb and shears had already been snatched from it. (446)

Typhon The son of Gaia (Earth) and Tartarus, a man-beast hybrid who was the strongest of all Earth's children. He had a hundred dragon's heads, but was human to the thighs, and had a coiled viper's tail and wings and feathers. Taller than any mountains, one hand reached to the west, the other to the east. Zeus fought a great battle with him and finally buried him under Etna. See also GIANTS. (103)

Ubastet The cat-goddess worshipped at Bubastos in Egypt; confused with the sacred lioness Pekhet, the Greeks identified her as Artemis, the Huntress. (490)

Uilebheist   A Gaelic monster of the deep with several heads. See SEA-
SERPENTS.   (509)

Unicorn   Of all beasts, fabulous or otherwise, Julius Solinus assures us
that 'the cruellest is the Unicorne, a Monster that belloweth horriblie,
bodyed like a horse, footed like an Elephant, tayled like a Swine and
headed like a Stagge. His horne sticketh out of the midds of his forehead,
of a wonderful brightness about foure foote long, so sharp, that whatsoever
he pusheth at, he striketh it through easily. He is never caught alive;
kylled he may be, but taken he cannot bee.'

If Solinus was embroidering the account given by Pliny in the first
century A.D., Pliny had in turn borrowed the story from Alexander the
Great's physician, Ctesias, who had travelled with the conqueror's armies
into Persia and India, and had seen or heard of wild asses there, which had
a single horn on their forehead about a foot and a half long, this horn being
a powerful antidote to poison.

The rarity of both the beast and its horn (though the latter was by no
means unknown) made it a favourite subject of medieval writers. It was
said to purify water by merely dipping its horn into it, and other beasts
around a drinking place would wait for the unicorn to arrive before they
quenched their thirst. As to its capture, the approved method was for a
virgin, preferably both beautiful and naked, to be bound to a tree; at
which the unicorn, attracted by a creature as rare and chaste as itself,
would approach, and meekly lay its head in her lap; and this would so
entrance it that it could easily be killed by the hunter waiting in ambush.
At one extreme, this became the allegory of the Holy Hunt, Christ being
the unicorn attracted by the Virgin Mary and slain for the sake of the
sinful world. At the other extreme, though this is by no means certain,
lies an Indian hunter's tale of a trick for capturing a rhinoceros by using a
specially trained female monkey which tickles and caresses that notori-
ously curmudgeonly beast into a sound sleep: this is at any rate as tall a
tale as the medieval means of taking unicorns.

Sir Thomas Browne, casting a cold eye over the whole affair, found
nothing but confusion: '*Pliny* affirmeth it is a fierce and terrible creature;
Vartomannus a tame and mansuete animal: those which *Garcias ab Horto*
described about the cape of good hope, were beheld with heads like
horses; those which *Vartomannus* beheld, he described with the head

of a deer; *Pliny, Ælian, Solinus,* and after these from ocular assurance, *Paulus Venetus* affirmeth, the feet of the *Unicorn* are undivided, and like the Elephants: But those two which *Vartomannus* beheld at *Mecha,* were as he describeth, footed like a Goat. As *Ælian* describeth, it is in the bigness of an Horse, as *Vartomannus,* of a Colt; that which *Thevet* speaketh of was not so big as an Heifer; but *Paulus Venetus* affirmeth, they are but little less then Elephants. Which are discriminations very material . . . What Horns soever they be which pass amongst us, they are not surely the Horns of any one kind of Animal, but must proceed from several sorts of *Unicorns.* For some are wreathed, some not: That famous one which is

preserved at St. *Dennis* near *Paris,* hath wreathy spires and cochleary turnings about it, which agreeth with the description of the *Unicorns* Horn in *Ælian.* Those two in the treasure of St. *Mark* are plain, and best accord with those of the *Indian* Ass, or the descriptions of other *Unicorns:* That in the Repository of the electour of Saxone is plain and not hollow, and is believed to be a true Land *Unicorns* Horn.' The chief source of such horns seems to have been the narwhal (see also MONOCEROS).

The rhinoceros is one possible source of the idea of a unicorn for no other one-horned mammals are known in nature except as the result of an accident – for instance, an antelope with one horn broken off – or of human interference, which has produced a kind of one-horned sheep and a one-horned bull, the latter by surgical transplanting of one horn bud and the removal of the other. It is Ctesias's original account that gives us the strongest clue: for in Persia there are both relief sculptures at Persepolis showing apparent unicorns (in fact antelopes with their horns in profile) and a Zoroastrian legend of a unicorn-creature. This is the three-legged ass (see ASS), whose horn dissipates 'all the vile corruption due to the efforts of noxious creatures', a creature whose exact symbolism remains doubtful. But he is a symbolic beast, and as such probably came originally from India. The Persians also spoke of a goat-unicorn, the Koresck, which they regarded as a pure and royal beast.

The unicorn's great enemy was the lion; so firmly was this believed that an early traveller in America, believing that there were unicorns there, deduced at once that there must be lions, on the principle that everything had its natural enemy. This rivalry is first described in the thirteenth-century letter of the fictitious Prester John: Topsell gives a paraphrase of the original: 'as soon as ever a Lion seeth a Unicorn, he runneth to a tree for succour, that so when the Unicorn maketh force at him, he may not only avoid his horn but also destroy him; for the Unicorn in the swiftness of his course runneth against a tree, wherein his sharp horn sticketh fast. Then when the Lion seeth the Unicorn fastened by the horn, without all danger he falleth upon him and killeth him.' Now the lion has very ancient connections with the sun, and the unicorn has a strong association with the moon, both of which are found in a wide variety of sources; and it is just possible that this is an echo of an ancient allegory of the sun putting the moon to flight.

At all events, the solitary, elegant, pure-white unicorn is one of the most alluring and mysterious of fabulous beasts, and it continues to catch the poet's imagination, as in Rilke's *Sonnets to Orpheus*, a poem which serves as both epitaph to the naturalist's unicorn and hymn to the living beast of the imagination:

This is the creature there has never been.
They never knew it, and yet, none the less,
they loved the way it moved, its suppleness,
its neck, its very gaze, mild and serene.

URUS

Not there, because they loved it, it behaved
as though it were. They always left some space.
And in that clear unpeopled space they saved
it lightly reared its head, with scarce a trace
of not being there. They fed it, not with corn,
but only with the possibility
of being. And that was able to confer
such strength, its brow put forth a horn. One horn.
Whitely it stole up to a maid, – to be
within the silver mirror and in her.

After which we may well say with Sebastian in *The Tempest*:

> *Now I will believe*
> *That there are unicorns.*

(And on the dangers of disbelief in unicorns see James Thurber, *The Unicorn in the Garden*.) See also ABATH, CH'I-LIN, MONOCEROS.

Unnati Bird-headed woman, wife of the divine GARUDA BIRD in Nepalese myth. (507)

Upland Trout American fish which nested in trees and flew well, but never entered the water. Tenderfoot lumberjacks were sent out to catch them. See FEARSOME CRITTERS. (412)

Urisk A shaggy, satyr-like spirit who haunted deserted places in the Highlands, particularly waterfalls. He helped farmers and was a kind of familiar spirit of farmsteads driven into the wild by Christianity. They would follow and terrify lonely travellers at night, but were harmless; and they were said to meet occasionally in great assemblies. Cf FUATH, POOKA. (514, 413)

Urus Another name for the Aurochs, but according to the bestiaries it was the largest of all creatures, bull-like, with saw-shaped horns. It drank seawater, and became intoxicated, attacking the earth with its horns, which it normally used to cut down trees. It was killed by hunters when its horns became entangled in thornbushes. Cf. APTALEON.   (204)

Vältar or **Vaettrar**   A favourable kind of NISSE who entered the house through drains; it was important not to pour boiling water down drains in case the vältar were in them.   (427)

Vamana   The fifth incarnation of the Hindu god Vishnu, a dwarf who could cover the entire universe in three strides.

Varaha   Vishnu's incarnation as a boar; in this guise he delivered the world from Hiranyaksha, who had carried off the earth to the depths of the ocean. The earth rests on his tusks, and earthquakes are caused by his shifting the burden from one tusk to the other. Compare AIDO HEVEDO, JINSHIN UWO and SESHA for mythical beasts as cause of earthquakes.   (470)

Varengan   A magic bird, swift as an arrow, whose feathers protected against curses and charms. It was the swiftest of all birds in Iranian myth.   (484)

Vegetable Lamb of Tartary (Barometz, Borametz or Jeduah)
A creature which was born a true animal and a living plant. According to medieval travellers there was a tree found in Tartary whose gourd-like fruit ripened to disclose a little lamb, perfectly formed, from whose fleece garments were woven. A more elaborate account described the lamb as growing on a flexible stem which allowed it to browse on the surrounding grass. When it had eaten everything in reach it died. It was a favourite

food of wolves; the flesh tasted of fish, the blood as sweet as honey. It is in fact a very distorted account of the cotton plant, whose vegetable wool baffled early western observers.   (218, 471)

Vishap   An Armenian dragon which lived on Mount Ararat; weapons dipped in its blood caused incurable wounds.   (485)

Vithafnir   The cock who stood on top of the Scandinavian world-ash Yggdrasil, glittering like gold, shining like lightning, on guard against the evil enemies of the tree. Also known as Gollinkambi.   (480)

Vörys-Mort   A giant found near the Volga, taller than the tallest tree, who rushed from place to place like a whirlwind, carrying men and animals with him. He was a good spirit, however, who showed huntsmen the way and drove game into a snare; in return, huntsmen offered tobacco to him.
                                                                   (482)

Vrtra   The dragon which encompassed the waters in Indian myth, repeatedly slain by Indra in order to release water and sunlight.   (484)

Vuokho   In Lapp belief, a giant evil bird of uncertain shape, source or plague and mosquitoes. Coleridge in *The Destiny of Nations* calls him:

'that Giant Bird
Vuokho, of whose rushing wings the noise
Is Tempest, when the unutterable Shape
Speeds from the mother of Death and utters once
That shriek, which never murderer heard, and lived.' (471)

Vyantaras In Indian Jain mythology, mischievous wood spirits. (484)

Water-Bull A small, black, hideous creature, soft and slippery, in appearance like a bull, which dwelt in lonely Scottish lochs. It mated with ordinary cattle, and its progeny had short ears. (509)

Water-Horse, Kelpie or **Nykur** Grey or black horse whose hooves pointed backwards; the tuft on its pastern was reversed. It could change shape at will; if it mated with an ordinary horse its offspring would always lie down in the water when crossing fords. It led men astray by enticing them to ride it across a river; if Christ's name was mentioned, they were dropped in the water. See also BOOBRIE. (427)

Wayzgoose Neither fabulous nor a beast, though it sounds like both: the printers' name for their annual union (or 'chapel') outing in the nineteenth century.

Were-Jaguar South American equivalent of a WEREWOLF.

Werewolves Wolves which were human beings in disguise, and which attacked other men. The ability to change shape could be either voluntary or involuntary, hereditary or acquired. The transformation could be effected by magical means, potions or by simply putting on an animal skin. The signs of a werewolf when in human shape were various: in Denmark, a man whose eyebrows met was believed to be one. If they were badly injured as wolves, they would become human again, still bearing the marks. Belief in werewolves or other were-creatures is very widespread. In Greece the idea is associated with Lycaon who sacrificed his son and turned into a wolf; if a man becomes a werewolf there, he will remain a wolf only for nine years as long as he does not eat human flesh, but if he does do so, his transformation is permanent. Werewolves are often sorcerers who deliberately assume the wolf's shape and power through a diabolical pact, a belief attached to were-jaguars, were-leopards in Africa, and similar creatures elsewhere. The reality of werewolves, as of vampires, is taken for granted in the Balkans; and even a distinguished council of theologians summoned by the Emperor Sigismund in the fifteenth century declared them to exist. Were-animals in other parts of the world have proved to be sorcerers dressed as animals, and a similar magical custom, dimly remembered, may also be at the base of the were-wolf tradition. (510)

Whale, Four-Footed This compound heraldic creature has a boar's head and tusks, four clawed feet, and rows of spikes on its body. The leonine whale has the general size and shape of a lion, with minute ears, a human face, scales on its body, and four lion's paws. (405)

Wild Huntsman The giant figure of Herne the Hunter, with a deer's head and antlers, was supposed to roam Windsor Park; he was probably a vague memory of a pagan deity.

Wild Men, *see* WODEWOSES

Wivre or **Guivre** This poisonous reptile, in form like a wingless dragon, which spread plagues, would flee from a naked man, but would attack anyone with clothes on. It is similar to the gargouille of Rouen; see also DRAGON. (209)

Wizard's Shackle, *see* BURACH-BHADI

Wodewoses or **Wild Men** These forest creatures, usually depicted as men with shaggy green hair all over their body, carrying clubs, are found as supporters in many coats of arms. In medieval times they were supposed to be semi-human beings who could not speak and were unable to control themselves when angry or lustful. It has been suggested that they were originally men suffering from a rare skin disease which causes a fur-like growth on the body; but they are more likely to be survivals from pagan beliefs. They abduct women and devour children, especially unbaptised children. Some wild men are one-eyed, and others are deformed ogres. Almost every medieval pageant had its wild man. In 1392

Charles VI of France and five other nobles dressed as wild men for a court festival in suits covered in pitch and flax. Despite special precautions, a torch was brought too close to one of the masquers, and four of the five courtiers, who were chained together in a circle, were burnt to death, the king only escaping because he was not tied to them.   (409)

Wonderful Pig of the Ocean   Heraldic sea-pig, with a quarter circle like a moon behind its head, dragon's feet, horns with eyes on each side, an eye in its belly and a fish tail.   (405)

Woodwives   Wood-spirits of many varying kinds, relics of pagan nature-worship. The male equivalents were less common, the German SCHRAT and the FAUN being two examples. Very often the woodwife was apparently beautiful, but from behind was either hollow or was like a tree-stump: in other forms they were at first old and ugly and then made themselves beautiful. They would appear to lonely travellers and take them as lovers, and then vanish. They were generally kind but unreliable;

they both caused and cured diseases, and offerings were left for them. Also called *Holzfrau, Iarnvithja, Ivithja, Löfriska, Mooseweibel, Skogsfru, Waldmännlein.* Cf ELLER WOMAN, VYANTARAS, WODEWOSES. (481)

Woolly Hens Sir John Mandeville describes hens in the Far East which have sheep's wool instead of feathers. (219)

Wyvern Flying serpent like a dragon, with two legs like an eagle's and a barbed tail; they are emblems of pestilence, but are frequently found in heraldry as a variant form of DRAGON. (515)

Xanthos, *see* BALIOS

Yahoos Deformed creatures encountered by Gulliver when he was abandoned on an unknown island while his ship was heading for Madagascar. Their heads and breasts were covered with thick hair, some frizzy, some lank, they had beards like goats and a long ridge of hair (sometimes brown or yellow or red or black) down their backs, and the fore parts of their legs and feet; the rest of the body was bare, showing a buff coloured skin, they had two tails. They frequently sat on the ground on their buttocks like humans; their buttocks were hairy, presumably for comfort's sake. They often stood on their hind legs. On their feet they had great claw hooks enabling them to scale trees with ease, and leap with extreme agility from one object to another. The females had only a down on their body, and their breasts hung down between their forelegs, almost touching the ground. They were very disagreeable, with hideously distorted faces and a habit of discharging their excrement in self-defence; they ate both meat and hay. Used as beasts of burden by the Houyhnhnms, who took Gulliver to be one of this species of animal, to his great chagrin.

Yale Originally a yali from southern India, a creature the size of a horse with a spotted body, an elephant's tail, boar's tusks and movable horns, it appears in heraldry as one of the Queen's beasts, and also in the arms of the Beauforts. In India it was placed in temples to guard against evil spirits. The EALE is an earlier version of the same beast found in the bestiaries. (474)

Yata Garasu Japanese three-legged crow, messenger of the gods; related to the magic crow, also three-legged, which lives in the sun according to the Chinese, where it causes sunspots. (463)

Yfrit An Arabian version of the griffin, or more commonly a spirit-being, one of the fallen angels.

Ylio A beast similar to the SALAMANDER. As with some accounts of the salamander, it is a lizard which can extinguish fire. (458)

Yllerions Prester John, in the letter supposed to have been written by him to the Christian princes of the west in the thirteenth century, describes yllerions as the lords of all birds, fire-coloured with plumes as sharp as razors. Only two live at any one time; they live for sixty years, and then lay two or three eggs, which they sit on for forty days before they hatch. The old birds then go to drown themselves in the sea, accompanied by all the other kinds of birds, which return to look after the young yllerions. This invented account relies heavily on the PHOENIX. (429)

Ypotains Half-man, half-horse; they sometimes lived on land, and ate only human beings. (219)

Ypotryll A type of heraldic dromedary or camel. (474)

Ysgithyrwyn A great boar pursued by Arthur in order to procure his tusk, so that the giant Ysbaddaden could shave with it before the wedding of his daughter Olwen to the hero Culhwch. See also TWRCH TRYWTH.

Ziphius A fish of monstrous size with an owl's head, horrible eyes, a wedge-shaped beak and a mouth like a huge pit. It marauded in northern waters, and was known to attack ships. It is neither the whale of the modern genus *Ziphius* nor the Greek *Xiphias*, a swordfish.

Ziz Gigantic bird of Hebrew myth, king of all birds; it is distantly connected with the ROC, the hen-ziz laying eggs of equally huge size.

(444)

Zû The storm dragon of Sumerian myth, who sought to rule the world and stole the tablets of fate on which the universal laws were written from the gods. Three gods refused to retrieve them, but Nimurta finally seized them from Zû's nest in the mountain of Sâbu. He is represented as a lion-headed eagle, or as an eagle grasping a lion, and is one of the cohorts of TIAMAT.

(483)

BIBLIOGRAPHY

I. PRE-CLASSICAL AND CLASSICAL (to A.D. 400)

101 AELIANUS, CLAUDIUS: *On the Characteristics of Animals*, tr. A. F. Scholfield (London and Cambridge, Mass. 1958–9)

102 APOLLODORUS: *The Library*, ed. and tr. J. G. Frazer (London and New York, 1921)

103 APOLLONIUS RHODUS: *The Argonautica*, ed. and tr. R. C. Seaton (London and New York, 1912)

104 ARISTOTLE: *Historia Animalium*, tr. D'Arcy Wentworth Thompson (Oxford, 1910)

105 CLAUDIAN: 'The Phoenix', tr. Henry Vaughan the Silurist in *Works*, ed. L. C. Martin (Oxford, 1927)

106 *Cuneiform Texts in the British Museum*, xvii 42 (London, 1907)

107 DIODORUS SICULUS: *Bibliotheca Historica*, tr. J. Skelton, ed. F. M. Salter and H. L. R. Edwards (*EETS* 233, London 1956–7)

108 *The Epic of Gilgamesh*, tr. N. K. Sandars (London and Baltimore, 1964)

109 HERODOTUS: *The Histories*, tr. A. de Selincourt (London and Baltimore, 1949)

110 HESIOD: *The Remains of Hesiod the Ascrean*, tr. C. A. Elton (London, 1815)

111 HOMER: *The Odyssey*, tr. E. V. Rieu (London and Baltimore, 1946)

112 HORAPOLLO NILUS: *The Hieroglyphics*, ed. and tr. A. T. Cory (London, 1840)

113 HYGINUS: *Fabulae*, ed. M. Schmidt (Jena, 1872)

114 LUCRETIUS: *On the Nature of the Universe*, tr. R. E. Latham (London and Baltimore, 1949)

115 OVID: *Metamorphoses*, ed. and tr. F. J. Muller (London, 1916)

116 PAUSANIAS: *Description of Greece*, ed. and tr. J. G. Frazer (London and New York, 1898)

117 PHILOSTRATUS: *The Life of Apollonius of Tyana*, ed. and tr. F. C. Conybeare (London and New York, 1912)

118 PLINY THE ELDER: *The Natural History of Pliny*, tr. J. Bostock and H. T. Riley (London, 1855)

119 SOLINUS, CAIUS JULIUS: *The Excellent and Pleasant Work of Julius Solinus Polyhistor*, tr. A. Golding (London, 1587)

120 STRABO: *The Geography*, tr. H. C. Hamilton and W. Falconer (London, 1854–7)

121 VIRGIL: *The Aeneid*, tr. W. F. Jackson Knight (London and Baltimore, 1956)

2. MEDIEVAL WESTERN (to A.D. 1500)

201 ALBERTUS MAGNUS: *B. Alberti Magni Opera Omnia XII: Animalium Libri XXVI*, ed. A. Bornet (Paris, 1891)

202 BARTOLOMAEUS ANGLICUS: *De Proprietatibus Rerum* (London, n.d.)

203 *Beowulf*, tr. Kevin Crossley-Holland (London, 1968)

204 CARLILL, J.: 'The Physiologus' in *The Epic of the Beast*, ed. W. Rose (London, 1924)

205 CARMODY, F. J.: 'Physiologus Latinus Versio Y' *University of California Publications in Classical Philology*, 12, 93–134 (Los Angeles, 1941)

206 CAXTON, WILLIAM: *Mirrour of the world*, ed. O. H. Prior (*EETS* E.S. CX, London, 1913)
CONTI, NICOLO D', *see* 223

207 COOK, A. S. and PITMAN, J. H.: 'The Old English Physiologus', *Yale Studies in English*, lxiii (Oxford and New Haven, 1921)

208 FIRDAUSÍ: *The Shahnámá of Firdausí*, tr. A. G. Warner and E. Warner (London, 1905)

209 FOURNIVAL, RICHARD DE: *Le Bestiaire d'amour*, ed. C. Hippeau (Paris, 1860)

210 GEOFFREY OF MONMOUTH: *History of the Kings of Britain*, tr. Lewis Thorpe (London and Baltimore, 1966)

211 GERVASE OF TILBURY: *Otia Imperialia*, ed. F. Liebrecht (Hanover, 1856)

212 GIRALDUS CAMBRENSIS: *The Historical Works*, tr. T. Forester and R. C. Hoare, rev. T. Wright (London, 1913)

213 GUILLAUME LE CLERC: *Le Bestiaire: das Thierbuch des normannischen Dichters Guillaume le Clerc*, ed. R. Reinsch (Leipzig, 1890)

214 HUGO DE SAINT-VICTOR: 'De bestiis' in *Opera omnia* in Migne, *Patrologia Latina* clxxvii, c. 13–164 (Paris, 1854)

215 ISIDORE OF SEVILLE: *Etymologiarum* in Migne, *Patrologia Latina* clxxxii c. 434–70 (Paris, 1850)

BIBLIOGRAPHY

216 JAMES, M. R.: *The Bestiary* (Roxburghe Club, Oxford, 1928)

217 *King Alisaunder*, ed. G. V. Smithers (*EETS* **227, 237,** London, 1952–7)

218 *Libellus de natura animalium*, ed. J. I. Davis (London, 1958)

219 'MANDEVILLE, SIR JOHN': *The Voyage and Travaile of Syr John Maundevile* (London, 1932)

220 NECKHAM, ALEXANDER: *De naturis rerum*, ed. T. Wright (Rolls Series 34, London, 1863)

221 PETER DAMIAN: 'De bono religioso status et variorum animantium tropologia' in Migne, *Patrologia Latina* cxlv c. 763–921 (Paris, 1835)

222 POLO, MARCO: *The Book of Ser Marco Polo*, tr. and ed. H. Yule, 3rd ed. rev. H. Cordier (London, 1926)

223 POLO, MARCO: *The Most Noble and Famous Travels Together with the Travels of Nicolo d'Conti*, tr. J. Frampton, ed. N. M. Penzer (London, 1937)

224 SAXO GRAMMATICUS: *Gesta Danorum*, tr. O. Elton (London, 1894)

225 THAUN, PHILIPPE DE: *Bestiary*, in T. Wright, *Popular Treatises on Science During the Middle Ages* (Historical Society of Sciences, London, 1841)

226 THEOBALDUS: *Bestiary*, tr. in R. Morris, *An Old English Miscellany* (*EETS* O.S. 49, London, 1872)

227 VINCENT DE BEAUVAIS: *Bibliotheca mundi*, bks. 16–20 (Antwerp, 1624)

228 WHITE, T. H.: *The Book of Beasts* (London, 1954)

229 WOLFRAM VON ESCHENBACH: *Parzival*, tr. E. H. Zeydel and B. Q. Morgan (Chapel Hill, 1951)

3. RENAISSANCE (1500–1700)

301 ALDROVANDUS: *Opera omnia*: de avibus; de quadrupedibus solidipedibus; de piscibus; de quadrupedibus digitatis; serpentum et dranconum historiae (Frankfurt and Bonn, 1611–1640)

302 ALLATIUS, LEON: *S. P. N. Eustathii in hexahemeron commentarius* (Lyon, 1629)

303 ARIOSTO, LUDOVICO: *Orlando Furioso* in English heroical verse by John Harington (London, 1594)

304 BODIN, JEAN: *Universae naturae theatrum* (Lyon, 1597)

305 BROWNE, SIR THOMAS: *Pseudodoxia epidemica* in *Works*, ed. C. Sayle (London, 1927)

306 BURTON, ROBERT (i.e. Nathaniel Crouch): *Miracles of Art and Nature* (London, 1676)

BIBLIOGRAPHY

307 DU BARTAS, GUILLAUME: *Du Bartes his Divine Weekes and Workes,* tr. Joshua Sylvester (London, 1612)

308 GESNER, CONRAD: *Historia animalium* (Frankfurt, 1585–1617)

309 GUILLIM, JOHN: *Display of Heraldry* (London, 1724)

310 HAKLUYT, RICHARD: *The Principal Navigations of the English Nation* (Glasgow, 1903–5)

311 HEYLIN, PETER: *Mikrokosmos, a Little Description of the Great World* (London, 1633)

312 *Hortus sanitatis* (Mainz, 1536)

313 HUON OF BORDEAUX: tr. Lord Berners, ed. S. L. Lee (*EETS* E.S. 40–1, 43, 50, London, 1882–7)

314 LEGH, GERARD: *Accedens of Armorye* (London, 1612)

315 LYCOSTHENES, CONRAD: *Prodigiorum ac ostentorum chronicon* (Basle, 1557)

316 MAGNUS, OLAUS: *Compendious History of the Goths, Swedes, and Vandals* (London, 1658)

317 *Malleus Maleficarum,* tr. Montagu Summers (London, 1928)

318 MALORY, SIR THOMAS: *The Works,* ed. E. Vinaver (Oxford, 1967)

319 PORTA, JOHN BAPTIST: *Natural Magick,* ed. D. J. Price (New York, 1957)

320 ROSS, ALEXANDER: *Arcana microcosmi* (London, 1652)

321 SWAN, JOHN: *Speculum mundi* (Cambridge, 1635)

322 TOPSELL, EDWARD: *The Historie of Foure-Footed Beastes* (London, 1607)

323 WOTTON, EDWARD: *De differentiis animalium* (Paris, 1552)

4. MODERN

401 ADELINE, JULES: *Les sculptures grotesques et symboliques* (Rouen, 1879)

402 ALLEN, JOHN ROMILLY: *Early Christian Symbolism in Great Britain and Ireland* (London, 1887)

403 ANDERSON, MARY DESIRÉE: *Animal Carvings in British Churches* (Cambridge, 1938)

404 ANDERSON, MARY DESIRÉE: *Imagery in British Churches* (London, 1955)

405 ASHTON, JOHN: *Curious Creatures in Zoology* (London, 1890)

406 BARING-GOULD, SABINE: *The Book of Werewolves* (London, 1865)

407 BARING-GOULD, SABINE: *Curious Myths of the Middle Ages* (London, 1877)

408 BERGER DE XIVREY, JULES: *Traditions teratologiques* (Paris, 1836)

BIBLIOGRAPHY

409 BERNHEIMER, RICHARD: *Wild Men in the Middle Ages* (London, 1952)

410 BORGES, JORGE LUIS and M. GUERRERO: *Manual de zoologia fantastica* (Mexico, 1957)

411 BORGES, JORGE LUIS and M. GUERRERO: *The Book of Imaginary Beings* (London, 1970)

412 BOTKIN, B. A.: *The American People* (New York, 1946)

413 BRIGGS, KATHERINE M.: *The Anatomy of Puck* (London, 1959)

414 BRODERIP, W. J.: *Zoological Recreations* (London, 1847)

415 BROWN, ROBERT, JR.: 'Remarks on the Gryphon, Heraldic and Mythological' in *Archaeologia*, 48, 355–78, 1885

416 BROWN, ROBERT, JR.: *The Unicorn: a Mythological Investigation* (London, 1881)

417 BROWN, W. J.: *The Gods had Wings* (London, 1936)

418 BULFINCH, THOMAS: *The Age of Fable* (London, 1927)

419 BURTON, MAURICE: *Phoenix Reborn* (London, 1959)

420 CAHIER, CHARLES: *Nouveaux mélanges d'archéologie, d'histoire et de littérature*, I: Curiosités mysterieuses (Paris, 1874)

421 CAHIER, CHARLES, and ARTHUR MARTIN: *Mélanges d'archeologie, d'histoire et de littérature* (Paris, 1847–56)

422 CAMPBELL, JOHN FRANCIS: *Popular Tales of the West Highlands*, iv (London, 1893)

423 CLAIR, COLIN: *Unnatural History* (London and New York, 1968)

424 CLARK, R. T. RUNDLE: 'Legend of the Phoenix' in *University of Birmingham Historical Journal*, 2, 1–140, 1949

425 COLLINS, A. H.: *Symbolism of Animals and Birds Represented in English Church Architecture* (London, 1913)

426 COTTRELL, LEONARD: *The Penguin Book of Lost Worlds* (London and Baltimore, 1962)

427 CRAIGIE, SIR WILLIAM: *Scandinavian Folklore* (London, 1896)

428 DAWSON, W. W. R.: *The Bridle of Pegasus* (London, 1930)

429 DENIS, FERDINAND: *Le Monde enchanté: cosmographie et histoire naturelle fantastique du moyen age* (Paris, 1843)

430 DONATUS, SISTER MARY: *Beasts and Birds in the Lives of Irish Saints* (Philadelphia, 1934)

431 DOUGLAS, NORMAN: *Birds and Beasts of the Greek Anthology* (London, 1928)

432 DRUCE, G. C.: 'The Caladrius and its Legend' in *Archaeological Journal*, 69 381–416, London, 1912

433 DUMÉZIL, GEORGES: *Le Problème des centaures* (Paris, 1929)

BIBLIOGRAPHY

434 DUMONT, LEON: *La Tarasque* (Abbeville, 1949)

435 ELLIOT-SMITH, G.: *The Evolution of the Dragon* (London, 1919)

436 ELLIOT-SMITH, G.: 'Dragons and Rain-Gods' in *Bulletin of the John Rylands Library* **5**, 317–80, Manchester, 1918–20

437 ELLIS DAVIDSON, H. R.: 'The Hill of the Dragon' in *Folklore* **61**, 169–85, 1950

438 ELLIS DAVIDSON, H. R.: *Gods and Myths of Northern Europe* (London, and Baltimore, 1964)

439 FOX-DAVIES, A. C.: *The Art of Heraldry* (Edinburgh, 1904)

440 GOULD, CHARLES: *Mythical Monsters* (London, 1886)

441 GOULD, M. M.: *Dragons and Sea-Serpents* (London, 1886)

442 GRAVES, ROBERT: *The Greek Myths* (London and Baltimore, 1951)

443 GRAVES, ROBERT: *The White Goddess* (London, 1948)

444 GRAVES, ROBERT and RALPH PATAI: 'Some Hebrew Myths and Legends' in *Encounter*, **20**, February–March 1963

445 'Gremlins, Aircrews, for the Use of' in *Punch*, 11 November 1942, 396

446 GUEST, LADY CHARLOTTE: *The Mabinogion* (London, 1902)

447 GUTCH, ELIZA: 'Saint Martha and the Dragon' in *Folklore* **63**, 193–203, 1952

448 HAMEL, FRANK: *Human Animals* (London, 1915)

449 HARTLAND, EDWIN SIDNEY: *The Legend of Perseus* (London, 1894–6)

450 HAUPT, MORIZ: *Liber monstrorum de diversis generibus* in *Opuscula* ii, 218–52 (Leipzig, 1876)

451 HENDERSON, GEORGE: *The Celtic Dragon Myth* (Edinburgh, 1911)

452 HERON-ALLEN, EDWARD: *Barnacles in Nature and in Myth* (London and New York, 1928)

453 HEUVELMANS, BERNARD: *On the Track of Unknown Animals*, tr. Richard Garnett (London and New York, 1958)

454 HEUVELMANS, BERNARD: *In the Wake of the Sea-serpents*, tr. Richard Garnett (London and New York, 1968)

455 HOPE, W. ST. JOHN: 'A Note on the Jall or Yale in Heraldry' in *Archaeological Journal*, **68**, 200–2, 1911

456 HUBAUX, JEAN and MAXIME LEROY: *Le Mythe du phénix dans les littératures grecque et latine*, Bibliotheque de la faculté de philosophie et lettres de l'universite de Liège, 82 (Paris, 1939)

457 HUGHES, M. Y.: 'Spenser's Blatant Beast', *Modern Languages Review*, xiii, 1918

458 HULME, F. E.: *Mythland* (London, 1886)

459 HULME, F. E.: *Natural History, Lore and Legend* (London, 1895)

BIBLIOGRAPHY

460 INGERSOLL, ERNEST: *Birds in Legend, Fable and Folklore* (London, 1923)

461 JANSON, H. W.: *Apes and Ape Lore in the Middle Ages and Renaissance* (London, 1952)

462 JEWITT, LLEWELLYN: 'The Dragon of Wantley and the Family of Moore' in *Reliquary* N.S. 18, 193–202, 1878

463 JOLY, H. L.: *Legend in Japanese Art* (London and New York, 1908)

464 KENNEDY, PATRICK: *Legendary Fictions of the Irish Celts* (London, 1891)

465 LANGE, CONRAD: *Der Papstesel* (Göttingen, 1891)

466 LANGLOIS, E. E.: *Stalles de la cathédrale de Rouen* (Rouen, 1838)

467 LAUCHERT, FRIEDRICH: *Geschichte des Physiologus* (Strassburg, 1899)

468 LAWSON, J. C.: *Modern Greek Folklore and Ancient Religion* (Cambridge, 1910)

469 LEACH, E. R.: 'St. George and the Dragon' in *Myth or Legend?*, ed. E. Glyn Daniel, 79–86 (London, 1955)

470 LEACH, MARIA, (ed.): *Standard Dictionary of Folklore, Mythology and Legend* (New York, 1949–50)

471 LEE, HENRY: *The Vegetable Lamb of Tartary* (London, 1887)

472 LEEMS, KNUD: *Beskrivelse over Finnmarkens Lapper* (Copenhagen, 1767)

473 LEY, WILLY: *The Lung fish and the Unicorn* (London, 1948; New York, 1949)

474 LONDON, HUGH STANFIELD: 'Minor Monsters' in *Coat of Arms*, 3–4 (7 parts) 1954–6

475 LOOMIS, R. S. (ed.): *Arthurian Literature in the Middle Ages* (London, 1959)

476 LOWER, MARK A.: *The Curiosities of Heraldry* (London, 1845)

477 LUM, PETER: *Fabulous Beasts* (London, 1952)

478 LUM, PETER: *The Stars in our Heaven* (London, 1951)
MACCULLOCH, JOHN ARNOTT, L. H. GRAY and G. F. MOORE (eds.): *The Mythology of All Races* (Boston, 1914–32)

479 I *Greek and Roman*: W. S. Fox

480 II *Eddic*: J. A. MacCulloch

481 III *Celtic*: J. A. McCulloch; *Slavic*: J. Machal

482 IV *Finno-Ugric, Siberian*: U. Holmberg

483 V *Semitic*: S. H. Langdon

484 VI *Indian*: A. B. Keith; *Iranian*: A. J. Carnoy

485 VII *Armenian*: H. M. Ananikian; *African*: A. Kerner

486 VIII *Chinese*: J. C. Ferguson; *Japanese*: M. Anesaki

BIBLIOGRAPHY

487 IX *Oceanic:* R. B. Dixon

488 X *North American:* H. B. Alexander

489 XI *Latin America:* H. B. Alexander

490 XII *Egyptian*: W. Max-Müller; *Indo-Chinese:* Sir J. G. Scott

491 MANSERGH, J. F.: 'The Salamander' in *Notes and Queries,* ser. 7, 10, 112, 1890

492 MENCKEN, H. L.: *The American Language,* Supplement I (New York, 1948)

493 PEACOCK, EDWARD: 'The Griffin' in *Antiquary* **10,** 89–92, 1884

494 PHIPSON, EMMA: *The Animal Lore of Shakespeare's Time* (London, 1883)

495 PONTOPPIDAN, ERIK: *The Natural History of Norway* (London, 1755)

496 RHYS, SIR JOHN: *Celtic Folklore, Welsh and Manx* (Oxford, 1901)

497 ROBIN, PERCY ANSELL: *Animals in English Literature* (London, 1932)

498 ROBINSON, H. S. and K. WILSON: *Encyclopaedia of Myths and Legends of All Nations* (London, 1962)

499 ROBINSON, PHILIP: *The Poet's Beasts* (London, 1885)

500 ROLT-WHEELER, ETHEL: 'Super-Animals in Poetry' in *Transactions of the Royal Society for Literature,* ser. 2, xxxiv, 47–86, 1916

501 ROSE, H. J.: *Handbook of Greek Mythology* (London, 1928)

502 SCHOEPPERLE, GERTRUDE: 'Le Morholt' in *Revue Celtique* **43,** 347–9, 1924

503 SÉJOURNÉ, LAURETTE: *El Universo de Quetzalcoatl* (Mexico and Buenos Aires, 1962)

504 SHAW, GEORGE BERNARD: 'The Chesterbelloc', *The New Age,* 15 February 1908

505 SHEPARD, ODELL: *The Lore of the Unicorn* (New York, 1930)

506 SIEBERT, JOHANNES: 'Ecidemon', *Zeitschrift für deutsche Philologie,* **62,** 1937, 248–64

507 SINGH, MADANJEET: *Himalayan Art* (London, 1968)

508 SPENCE, LEWIS: *The Gods of Mexico* (London, 1923)

509 SPENCE, LEWIS: *The Magic Arts in Celtic Britain* (London, 1945)

510 SUMMERS, MONTAGU: *Werewolves* (London, 1933)

511 TATLOCK, J. S. P.: 'The Dragons of Wessex and Wales' in *Speculum* xviii, 223–35, 1933

512 THOMPSON, STITH: *Motif-index of Folk Literature* i, B. 0–99 (Copenhagen, 1955–8)

513 TONGUE, RUTH L. (ed.): *Forgotten Folk-Tales of the English Counties* (London, 1970)

514 TRISTRAM, H. B.: *The Natural History of the Bible* (London, 1867)

BIBLIOGRAPHY

515 VINYCOMB, JOHN: *Fictitious Creatures in Art* (London, 1906)

516 WATKINS, M. G.: *Gleanings from the Natural History of the Ancients* (London, 1885)

517 WAUGH, ARTHUR and GWEN BENWELL: *Sea Enchantress* (London, 1961)

518 WERNER, E. T. C.: *Myths and Legends of China* (London, 1924)

519 WILHELM, RICHARD (ed.): *Chinese Folktales*, tr. E. Osers (London, 1971)

520 WOOSNAM-JONES, W. E.: 'Gremlins' in *Spectator*, 1 January 1943, 7–8

521 *Notes and Queries*: ser. 1, 2, 517, 1850; ser. 1, 12, 31–3, 1845; ser. 3, 7, 7, 75, 210, 230, 1865; ser. 3, 9, 158–60, 1866; ser. 4, 7, 478, 1873

5. BIBLIOGRAPHIES

ROBINSON, MARGARET W.: *Fictitious Beasts* (Library Association Bibliographies, 1, London, 1961)

There are also full bibliographies in nos. 227 (sometimes inaccurate) and 422, 453, 454

ACKNOWLEDGEMENTS

The editor and publishers would like to thank the following who have kindly given permission for the use of copyright material: George Allen & Unwin Ltd, for the extract from *Iphigenia in Tauris* by Gilbert Murray; Gerald Duckworth & Co. Ltd, for 'The Microbe' from *Cautionary Verses* by Hilaire Belloc; Victor Gollancz Ltd, for the extract from Lewis Thorpe's translation of *The History of the Kings of Britain* by Geoffrey of Monmouth (1966); Hogarth Press Ltd, for the extract from J. B. Leishman's translation of Rilke's *Sonnets to Orpheus*.